Praise for Cristi Bundukamara's

Pain & Purpose:
My Journey to Mental Strength

"In a beautiful love letter to her children, Dr. Cristi Bundukamara shares words of wisdom and her heartfelt journey to find mental strength."

—Charlene Walters, MBA PhD, Business Mentor and Author

"If you have ever complained about things in your life, read this book and you never will again. This is the unbelievably powerful, heartbreaking, yet inspirational true story of the amazing Bundukamara family. It is a profoundly moving testament to the power of faith, hope and love in the face of ongoing obstacles and tragedy. You will finish, moved to try to follow their example."   **—Patrick Collin**

"This book is full of incredible wisdom, beautiful transparency, and raw truth. Thank you for sharing this incredibly difficult and challenging life you have had and also sharing the blessings and strength you have revived throughout it all."   **—Dara Lightle**

"This book is wonderful. She shares many personal heartbreaking experiences in a way that as the reader you feel the growth from the amazing healing experience. When tragedy strikes, nothing seems possible to take away the pain. But with understanding your own feelings, you realize your greatest strengths. This book is amazing!"

—Lisa Classen

Pain & Purpose

My Journey to Mental Strength

Also by
Discover the Mentally STRONG Method

You Can Heal After Tragic Loss:
A 45 Day Guidebook to Controlled Grief

Raising Mentally STRONG Kids:
A curriculum for building confident mentors,
teachers, parents and ultimately kids

Pain & Purpose

My Journey to Mental Strength

Cristi Bundukamara

EdD PMHNP

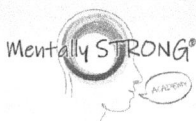

PUBLISHED BY
MS Expansion Enterprise Inc

To all who've known pain
but found strength and purpose.
This book is dedicated to you,
resilient souls.
Your journey inspires us all.

Contents

Acknowledgements

I would like to express my deepest gratitude to all the people in my life who believed in me, even when I did not believe in myself. The following individuals and organizations have played a significant role in the creation and realization of this memoir. Your support, encouragement, and contributions have been invaluable:

My sister, Jada, thank you for your support throughout this journey. Your belief in me sustained me through the highs and lows of writing my memoir.

The leadership team, Heather, Kim and Tara, and the rest of the incredible staff at Mentally STRONG. Thank you for believing in my mission to empower all humanity to embrace the journey of mental strength.

Charlene Walters, your willingness to read early versions of my manuscript and provide honest feedback was invaluable. Your fresh perspectives helped me see my story in new ways. Your insightful comments and suggestions contributed significantly to the overall quality of this memoir. Your meticulous editing skills helped make this memoir the best it could be. Thank you for your time and dedication.

Mara Purl at Haven Books, LLC, Thank you for believing in my story and helping me navigate the complex world of publishing. Your expertise and advocacy were crucial in bringing this memoir to a wider audience.

Everyone who read the early versions of this memoir, followed my story and my progress, and offered words of encouragement on social media and beyond, thank you for being a part of this journey.

With heartfelt appreciation,

Cristi Bundukamara

My Why

My reason for sharing the details of my personal journey is in the earnest hope that processing my story will help to heal some of my emotional pain, dissolve my initial anger at God, heal my broken heart, and allow me to say with confidence that I am Mentally STRONG. Additionally, I deeply wish that you will be inspired and encouraged by my story. In the midst of my hardships, I learned how to develop my mental strength through processing, organizing, making positive decisions, and never giving up. I hope to help you (and many others) to say, "I am Mentally STRONG."

Every good story has a hero, a problem, a plan, and hopefully an inspirational guide. The guide encourages a call to action and helps you avoid failure. Although I am the main character in this story, I want you to imagine yourself in your own life story and ask yourself the following questions: What kind of joy, peace, or happiness do I long for? Who or what is stopping me from having what I want? What will my life look like if I do (or do not) get what I want? My hope is that this book allows you to see me not as a victim or a hero, but as an inspirational guide to your own success, and the Mentally STRONG Method as your action plan.

If I, Cristi Bundukamara, can continue to find happiness amongst the most tragic losses, you can find your happiness too. I want my story to empower you to learn that the joy, peace, and happiness you desire come from within. And like me, the only thing stopping you from getting what you want is your own negative internal dialogue. We all experience it. Mine sounds something like this: I am not good enough…I am not smart…I can't pay attention long enough to write a book…People will judge me…I didn't do enough…I will work my hardest but still won't be successful. But I have learned to turn that negative thinking around. I'm confident that you will, too, as you grow in mental strength as I have done over the years.

It has been quite a journey. When I was first married, I faced the usual struggles that most young couples encounter but felt ready for the challenge. Over time, my family grew, and my heart did too. My diverse household included myself, my husband (Bundy), two biological mixed-race children, and five adopted children. With each new addition, I felt lucky and blessed. I believed that God had a special plan for me, but when a senseless tragedy and a devastatingly rare and difficult-to-diagnose genetic disorder struck my family, it challenged my view of life, my mental strength, and my faith in God.

It goes without saying, of course, that life is filled with joy and pain, in varying degrees, for everyone. But, if I'm being honest, I feel that I've had more than my fair share of both. Do I feel singled out? Sometimes. Have I ever wallowed in my grief and felt sorry for myself? Yes. Have I ever gotten permanently stuck there? No. With each new blow, I've found a way to move forward, process my thoughts, and make the choice to keep going. Through my experiences and those of the many clients I've worked with over the years, I recognize that people are immensely resilient. We all have the choice to find mental strength, to love, to hope, to persevere, and to never give up.

I am a devoted follower of Christ, and while the important foundation my faith has given me will be reflected in my writing, this book is not an explicitly Christian work by any means. My story is not an attempt to proselytize for converts. It is a human story, easily embraced by all people, no matter what their religious beliefs. While I talk about my relationship with God, it is merely *my* journey. You don't have to relate to everything. You are simply invited to share in the triumphs and struggles, and to (hopefully) learn from my experience. I came up with the title, *Pain & Purpose: My Journey to Mental Strength,* to reflect two major themes. The first is that each one of us must choose to find purpose in our pain. The second is that we all have, deep within, this amazing ability to overcome life's worst moments. It's our personal responsibility to persist and rise to the challenges. The idea of mental strength has given me the assurance that we *can* truly choose our state of mind and govern our emotions. Choosing this mindset has also enabled me to face each day with the peace needed to make difficult emotional decisions. The second notion has shown me that we are given the strength to persevere when we seem to be facing impossible odds. My determined refusal to give up in times of great stress and adversity has been a key factor in keeping me (and my family) focused on what must be accomplished, rather than giving in to paralyzing fear.

As a result of my own personal struggles, I developed a self-help technique called The Mentally STRONG Method, which I first used on myself. The Mentally STRONG Method is a simple and practical method for boosting your mental strength. It empowers you to organize your thought processes and develop a personal algorithm for perseverance. If you are interested in learning about The Mentally STRONG Method, visit *www.MentallyStrong.com*.

I am Cristi Bundukamara and this is my story.

No matter your story,

you can choose strength,

and eventually, joy.

—Dr. B

CHAPTER ONE

Tragedy Strikes

My adoptive father's family held an annual reunion in Kentucky, which I enjoyed attending every year as a young girl. I had such fond memories of the delicious food, abundant laughter, and heaps of cousins everywhere. I hadn't been back since marrying Bundy, though, because I was worried about how we'd be perceived. My father's side was a very white, country family, and although I didn't remember any racist behavior in my youth, I was concerned that there might be offensive remarks or behavior directed at my interracial family. We had lived through a difficult year with our recently adopted children, and I didn't want to put them through any more unpleasantness. Despite my misgivings, I still longed to attend the r eunion. It had been a while for me, and I missed my extended family.

I weighed the pros and cons, and ultimately, the little girl in me won the debate. I packed up the family, and we embarked on the long journey to Kentucky. It was just the seven of us: Reggie and Miah, our biological children; Johnny, Cristina, and Kayla, the three-child sibling group we had been called to adopt; and

Bundy and me. Our other adopted children, Cory and Nidra, were older and decided not to join us on the trip. Although we'd been through some challenges leading up to that moment, we were actually, unbeknownst to me, still in our family's honeymoon years (the best times). I could not have known what lay in store for us and that this trip would be the tipping point for a downward spiral.

After traveling for what seemed like forever, we pulled up at a beat-up, old gas station in the tiny town of Stearns, Kentucky. We piled out of the van, the seven of us, hoping to stretch our legs and fill up the tank. An elderly gentleman immediately hobbled over to us. In this small town it seemed as though we had stepped back in time; they still had an employee that pumps the gas for you. "I'm Gus, how much gas do you need?" he said, extending a worn hand to shake Bundy's before reaching for the pump. Then, in a strange yet encouraging gesture, he offered Bundy a Yoo-Hoo chocolate drink.

Thinking that perhaps Gus had just been a particularly friendly person, I was surprised when we received the same kind of reception in the Stearns grocery store. Now, Bundy is the kind of guy who talks to everybody, but when another random stranger struck up a conversation with him, it seemed like more than a fluke. Contrary to my fears, I hadn't detected even a hint of racism in this little town. We felt supported and welcomed, embraced even. When I mentioned that we'd come for the Ross family reunion, they all knew exactly whom I meant. The welcome we were getting made us feel silly that we'd avoided Kentucky for so many years. I had misjudged these friendly people.

My adoptive dad's parents grew up in Stearns, a small mining town. The small house where the reunions are held has been in my family for generations, and it's situated on a hill about a mile from the Big South Fork of the Cumberland River, just outside the Big South Fork National River and Recreation Area. It was strange for me to attend the reunion for the first time as an adult. My dad's parents had lots of brothers and sisters who would all come together with their extended families, somewhere between thirty to fifty family members in total— aunts, uncles, distant cousins—most of whom no longer lived in Kentucky.

There was only enough space for a few people inside the tiny house. Others stayed with local relatives or in hotels and cabins. Sometimes families would set up campsites in the large field surrounding the house—it was a sight. Like many of the others, we also established our home base for the reunion in that field and felt relaxed, enjoying the festive, vacation atmosphere. We spent time mingling and chatting with our extended family while barbequing that first evening. Bundy and I felt so relieved at how the day had unfolded. When it was time to retire, we slept well, looking forward to the next day at the river. It was a place where children could paddle in the shallows and the older children and adults could swim or kayak at their leisure. The whole family was excited for the fresh air and fun.

The bright sun woke us up early that next morning, and we loaded about ten people and a stack of tubes into the back of a pickup truck that was headed toward the river. The rubber tubes jostled as we drove along. My cousin Steven, always a prominent figure at the reunion, led the charge—it just wouldn't be a reunion without Steven. Steven and I were really close as children even though he was a few years younger than me. We would often go rock climbing and on other adventures. I remember rappelling down huge waterfalls with him and laughing until it hurt while getting completely soaked. Steven was the life of the party—always fun to be with and really active. This reunion was no different.

The lazy afternoon was spent relaxing by the river and keeping an eye on the kids. Reggie and Miah were laughing and splashing in the shallows near the water's edge. The kids all really seemed to be enjoying themselves. Cristina and Kayla, the charismatic sisters, were catching some sun on the sandy bank lining the river. Their big brother, Johnny, was bonding and swimming with his newfound cousins, a group of teenage boys roughly his own age. Johnny wasn't a very strong swimmer, so I insisted that he wear a life jacket, which probably didn't feel very cool to him at the time. They were being boisterous, splashing and wrestling as teen boys often do.

The eddy hole, as we all called it, was the section of the river where we always swam. It was wide and very deep. An eddy is an area in a river where the water slows down and creates a circular current that makes the water seem very still and serene. When I was a child, I heard colorful stories about how endless that eddy hole was. The way it was told to me, no one had ever been able to reach the bottom. The older folk would tease us saying, "Be careful! Don't go in too deep. There are 300-pound catfish waiting there to get you!" I could picture them, gray and ferocious, and knew for sure that I didn't want to mess with them. It was all in good fun though. No one had ever gotten hurt at the eddy hole.

Just a tiny bit tanner and a good bit happier, we returned home from our first day on the river. It was another pleasant evening intermingling with our big family on the lawn. I looked over at Miah. Her curls were bouncing as she laughed with Reggie. Cristina and Kayla were pulling roasted marshmallows off sticks, and Johnny was stretched out on a lawn chair next to the other boys, downing a can of cola. Each wore wide smiles on their faces. I felt so thrilled that my children were having so much fun.

Bundy and I discussed our plans for the next day. Since Bundy doesn't feel comfortable swimming, he decided that he would stay at the house and relax. He would be much happier sitting on the porch with Reggie and the girls anyhow. Johnny wanted to hang out with the other boys at the eddy hole again. I wanted to do something different, so Steven and I arranged to go on a kayaking adventure. We would start about two miles upriver and kayak down to meet everyone else at the eddy hole.

We all had breakfast together before Steven and I loaded up the kayaks in the back of a pickup truck. I waved goodbye to Bundy, Cristina, Kayla, Reggie, and Miah, who were sitting in a circle on the porch. The summer heat was sweltering, and I could hear the June bugs buzzing in the nearby grass. Johnny jumped into the back of a different pickup truck with his new friends, laughing and chatting it up. It was so good to see my boy relaxed and just being a typical teenager. For the moment, he had discarded his painfully shy exterior, which was wonderful to witness. I caught Johnny's eye and waved. His face lit up, and he waved back at me. The pickup was now overflowing with excited boys and rubber tubes. I saw Steven's wife and another woman, the mother of two boys, loading the front of the pickup with food and drinks for the day at the river. They would be supervising the rowdy group. Steven's wife waved to us as we took off down the dirt road toward the river.

It was a gorgeous day, and I grinned as we navigated the wooded roads. We'd made the right decision after all. Kentucky was beautiful, and the kids and I were soaking it all in. Steven knew this section of the river intimately, having spent most of his life hiking, swimming, and kayaking the Big South Fork of the Cumberland River. The sunlight seemed to be dancing on the water, reflecting onto the trees on the opposite bank. The effect was magical as it created a wash of sparkling light on the canopy of leaves. Steven grinned. "We've missed you at our reunions these past few years. It's good to have you and your family here with us," he acknowledged in his smooth Kentucky drawl. He pulled a red and white kayak off the pickup and heaved it over to me. "It's good to be here," I replied sincerely. The truth was that I felt more content than I had in a while. I settled into the shallow seat of my kayak, and we pushed off from the bank.

Our paddles splashed as we navigated the current, working our way downstream. Surrounded by the beauty of nature, I relished the feel of my muscles working. My mind drifted freely, resting on how blessed my life was. I had married a really good man who loved me. I had seven beautiful children. I couldn't have asked for more.

The sun was higher in the sky when I first heard the growl of an engine. I scanned the area in an attempt to identify the source of the sound. It seemed to be coming from the direction of a park ranger who stood on a large rock near the bank. "Get off the river!" he shouted to us. Steven frowned and shook his head at me. "Something's wrong. They don't do this." I wondered what could be happening. "Our family is downriver," yelled Steven, as we navigated to the bank and followed his instructions, "what's going on?" The ranger just shrugged. We were probably about a mile from the eddy hole, but Steven immediately broke into a run.

A sense of foreboding hung thick in the air. "Wait here. I'll send somebody back for you," Steven called out to me over his shoulder. I passed the time, biting my nails and fiddling with my hands for what seemed like forever, until my Uncle Allen came for me in a truck. "I don't know how to tell you this, Cristi," he said, "but Johnny's gone missing." *What did he mean by missing?* I rattled off several rapid-fire questions until Allen responded with one of the most painful things that I'd ever heard. "They told me that he was trying to swim across the river with the rest of the boys but started struggling…" I held my breath. "And went under before anyone could get close enough to help." What? That could not be true! Tears welled up in my eyes, and my heart nearly pounded out of my chest. No, not Johnny, whom we were only just getting to know. Not the sweet boy who was just coming out of his shell. The panic engulfed me, and my thoughts turned to his sisters, Cristina and Kayla. *I've got to get to the girls! Surely Johnny would have worn his life jacket before crossing the river.* I prayed that he had put that life jacket on.

I flew out of the truck and ran down to the bank to see what was happening. It was worse than I could ever have imagined.

There were rescue divers in the water and paramedics everywhere. The intensity seemed to be increasing. They had not found him yet. *Please find him*, I prayed. *PLEASE FIND HIM!* I craned my neck to locate him, hoping to catch a glimpse of him…to see some kind of sign. *Come on, Johnny! Please.*

Before long, Bundy and the girls joined me on the bank. We huddled together, crying in a desperate heap. Steven was still diving, searching frantically for Johnny in the bottomless depths. I knew Steven. He wasn't going to give up. He kept diving and kept trying. *Please find Johnny, Steven. Please… find…Johnny.* My mind became flooded with stories about how deep that spot was and how no one had ever been to the bottom. *Please don't be at the bottom, Johnny.*

Bundy was terrified, but even at this seemingly hopeless moment, he kept praying. I continued to stare into the light brown river water, desperately trying to see through the murk in the hope of sighting Johnny. Try as I might, I couldn't see through it, and I knew that Steven and the other divers were facing a very difficult task. I tried to remain hopeful, holding Cristina and Kayla, while Bundy prayed feverishly for the safe return of our son.

My hope eventually began to crumble against the reality of the situation. Johnny had disappeared underwater at least twenty minutes before I'd arrived. As a nurse, I didn't like the math. I knew that such a long amount of time really limited Johnny's chance of survival, even if they could locate him. It began to sink in that they may never find Johnny… I might never share another laugh or smile with him or watch him grow up. I might not witness his many joys and triumphs. I couldn't believe this could happen on what was meant to be a fun family trip. Why? It didn't make any sense. I looked over at the girls. After all they had already been through, this seemed so terribly unfair. I had promised them that they would all be safe. The three siblings. They had *us* now. Shouldn't they have been safe?

We shivered on that bank for many hours until one of the divers finally found Johnny. The diver emerged from the water holding Johnny's lifeless body. The sight was surreal. I stepped outside of myself; I could see the whole scene unfolding. The pain was too much. I just couldn't believe that God had allowed this. How could He do this to us, particularly Cristina and Kayla. Hadn't they already had enough adversity? This was a searing bolt from out of the blue. Within a few hours, we were all on the road home—without Johnny. I could not fathom it. Johnny was not coming home with us today or ever.

CHAPTER TWO

Long Drive Home

I drove straight through the night. I felt so alone with my deafening thoughts in that silent car. Why us? We were good people. Where had we gone wrong? My mind drifted back on my journey as a young wife and mother. During those early years, we thrived, with everything seeming to fall into place. I knew Bundy and I were soulmates, mostly because I could feel God's love through him. I always believed that if we continued doing good and obeying God, He would continue to bless us in every area—spiritually, physically, and emotionally.

Life was great for a while, although not always easy. Bundy became a full-time teacher and football coach at the local high school. He excelled as a teacher and a coach, and his team went nine years undefeated. Both his winning streak and ability to form mentoring relationships with the teens solidified him as a favorite in the community.

I had been doing really well, too, personally, professionally, and spiritually. Having built such a strong base, we wanted to move forward in our lives. I was in church on Mother's Day, when a message on the value of a mother's contributions really touched my heart. Bundy and I decided that very day to stop taking birth control with one goal in mind, to become parents! And lucky me, I got pregnant within a few months. Pregnancy is a wonderful, challenging, and often stressful time for any soon-to-be-parent, and it was the same for us. I loved being pregnant, though, observing my growing belly. We did everything that new parents do—I watched what I ate, heeded the doctor's advice, and attended all my appointments. We were overjoyed when we found out that we were expecting a boy. I was certain that he—our little baby boy—was going to be a perfect addition to our lives! And so, he was. Our Reggie was born on May 5, 1999, a flawless little boy.

Only parents can know the delight of holding a beautiful little person who reflects both of you, and yet is still his own little individual self. Just as during the pregnancy, we wanted to do everything right. I kept striving to be a good mother and decided to stay home to nurse Reggie and provide everything that he needed. I felt so blessed. Reggie was a healthy, active child who brought endless joy to our hearts and developed normally according to all the milestones for his age. I was so confident and assured of God's leading and protection in our lives that we dedicated Reggie to God in the covenant of baptism. I was awed by the depth and power of that moment of complete spiritual submission to God. I fully believed in His protection and blessing over our precious son.

I loved being a mom and wanted to keep it going. When Reggie was only a year old, we welcomed our beautiful daughter, Miah, into the world on May 1, 2000. I couldn't have felt more blessed with such a perfect addition to our family. She was just as delightful as Reggie. We now had one of each, a boy and a girl, just under a year apart. I was thrilled and basked in the delight of young motherhood.

My focus shifted back to the present as I stared vacantly at the road ahead. Those times seemed so far away now. Here I was driving home without one of the children that I had grown to love so much, driving home without my Johnny. I couldn't believe it and canvassed my mind for answers, drifting inward again.

It just wasn't right. I had dedicated my life to God, and He didn't protect my family. Bundy and I were even missionaries with *Mission to the World*. We were elated when we were chosen to do the work that God had called us to do. Most of it involved planning and organizing trips locally, but Bundy and I were also sent on international expeditions. As soon as we began, we knew that we were in God's perfect will. The international trips involved training locals to first find a house in the community. The house was then equipped like a family home and opened up to homeless children every day for breakfast, showers, clean clothes, Bible study, and lunch. This provided them with a place to hang out, receive meals, and make use of the facilities when needed. The ultimate goal was to teach them about Christ and His love for them, get them off the street, and usually to get them off drugs in the process. It was so rewarding to make a difference in their lives and to help where we were needed.

At that time, once again, I'd counted my blessings. What more could any young mother have asked for? I'd found my soul mate in marriage, we had delightful children in a loving home, and our whole family worked as a team in our calling to help others. These were "the honeymoon years."

I looked up and saw red lights flashing in my rear-view mirror followed by a loud siren. I must have been speeding. Ugh! Didn't he realize that I just wanted to get home? I glanced at myself in the mirror. I looked like a battered wife. I'd been up all night driving, and my eyes were red and swollen. The officer asked me to get out of the car and motioned me toward the back of the vehicle. "Ma'am, are you alright?" he asked, eyeing all the kids in the back and then Bundy. "My son just died," I cried, falling to the ground. I was on the verge of hysteria. The officer gave me a fatherly pat and asked Bundy to get out of the car. "Sir," he said, "I believe you need to take over the drive." And Bundy did.

I was in the passenger's seat now, but my mind kept steering. I thought about the day we'd adopted Johnny, Kayla, and Cristina—our precocious three-child sibling group. That morning, I'd heard the phone vibrate before it rang. My heart began to race when I saw that the call was from Child Protective Services. *Is this it?* I recognized the case worker's voice right away. "We have a twelve-year-old boy here. He has no problems, and in fact, he looks like he could be your biological child."

A smile stretched across my face. It had been going so well with Nidra and Cory, our two previously adopted children, that Bundy and I felt called to continue adopting children who needed a loving home. We knew both Nidra and Cory personally before adopting them. We knew their lives and their stories. They were appreciative of the opportunity to become a part of our family, and their behavior reflected that. We wanted a large family but weren't certain of the exact number of children. Our plan was to adopt one child at a time over the course of a few years and see where God led us.

"Oh, and one other thing," the case worker added, "he has nowhere to sleep tonight." A requirement of potential foster parents is to have a room prepared for the child to sleep in. Bundy and I had specified that we wanted to adopt only boys as Bundy felt better equipped to raise boys based on his experience. Overjoyed, we tried to quell our nervous excitement and physically and emotionally prepare before leaving to pick up our new son.

With bated breath, we followed the case worker into a small room to meet Johnny. I remember first laying eyes on him. He was about five feet five, around a hundred pounds, and had a clear, light brown complexion. I was confused because he was sitting on the bench with two younger girls. They were all huddled together like a pack. Johnny's gaze was guarded, somewhat apprehensive, as the case worker introduced us. I smiled at him warmly in an attempt to reassure him and then turned my smile toward the girls.

"Those are his sisters," the caseworker remarked casually. "The three of them have never been separated before. The girls have nowhere to go either." She went on to tell me that the trio had been returned to foster care earlier that day by their previous adoptive mother, who, without any warning, stated that she simply couldn't do it anymore. It astounded me that a person could tell children that she loved them, let them call her mom, and then return them.

We were prepared for only one child, but how could we separate Johnny from his sisters and leave the girls there? Our envisioned strategy was to adopt a string of boys, each one settling in before adopting the next. We'd pictured a cheerful

little football team running around the house but were to learn
that our plans are not always God's plans. Trusting in God, we
decided to adopt Johnny *and* his two sisters. Cristina was ten,
and Kayla was nine. They were three of nine children born to
parents who were substance abusers. They'd lived in multiple
foster homes, some worse than others, through the Miami foster
care system.

The three children each had their own individual person-
alities. Johnny was a sweet boy with a distinctly male sense of
humor and a knack for drawing. Shy and withdrawn, he was
guarded and kept a safe distance between himself and other
people. He seemed content living with us, however, and got
along particularly well with Reggie. It was often more difficult
to read him though. His sister Cristina, on the other hand, was
more openly anxious and worried about everything. She was a
cute girl, and her beautiful, cream-brown skin highlighted the
mole above her left cheekbone. Kayla, the youngest of the three,
was very different from both of her siblings. She was animated,
loud, and very happy. Kayla was always right there in the mix
of things, and very strong-willed, even as a child. She could be
downright rebellious at times—just as I was at that age.

I don't know if we would have agreed to accept all of the
children if we had been told that there were three. Perhaps
we had been slightly manipulated by the case worker. Maybe
she thought that if we saw them all together, it would pull on
our heartstrings. And it did. Whatever her intentions were, it
worked. And you know what? Taking in all three kids made
me feel powerful. Because I am a psychiatric nurse practitioner
and Bundy a special needs teacher, I felt we were better prepared

for it than most. God had already equipped us for raising challenging and emotionally demanding children. I believed that if we covered them in love and applied discipline, they would respond and grow into the adults they were meant to be. I felt we were unstoppable and that we would be able to handle anything thrown at us.

The feeling of being unstoppable began to diminish within months of having Johnny and his sisters in our home. I had initially judged the woman who had returned them to Child Protective Services, but within three months of living with them, I understood her decision. Even though I had Bundy, my mom, and a family support system, I was struggling—there was no way a single, retired woman would have been able to manage it. When their behavioral problems emerged during that first year, Child Protective Services let us look at some previous reports on the children. After reading those reports, it became clear that they had not been truthful when they told us the children were problem-free. Through counseling and conversations, each one started to reveal more and more about what they'd been through, and it was a tremendous amount.

I quickly found out that it wasn't as easy as raising them by applying love and discipline. They're trauma was so severe that they had intense attachment issues. I was naïve to believe that our training had prepared me to manage the effects of such deep-seated trauma. Ultimately, it was our tenacity and the determined choice not to give up that kept us going. Children with reactive attachment disorder are not bad children. The disorder subconsciously tells them that they are not worthy of love. Sadly, Johnny, Cristina, and Kayla had been returned to

Child Protective Services twice before by adoptive parents who found their behavior too challenging to deal with.

It was a tough road, and that first year with them was exceptionally difficult. We consistently tried to show them that we did truly love them and did our best to assure them that they were now, and always would be, part of a forever family. It became clear that convincing them was not going to be as easy as it had been with Nidra and Cory. We thought they'd get along well with each other, but they fought constantly. Any attempt at discipline caused conflict. When asked to do simple chores, they would threaten to call Child Protective Services and (falsely) report abuse. Still, we did our best to allow them the freedom to complain and protest but continued to apply the discipline they needed. At times, I admit, I felt underappreciated and discouraged at their lack of gratitude. I understood their reluctance to accept our love after having been bounced around so much, but still, we were offering them real love in our home with our family.

Theirs was a sad story. Johnny, Cristina, and Kayla were removed from their mother's custody due to her substance abuse and subsequent neglect a number of times. Soon after the last sibling was born, they were taken away for good. The children's grandmother cared for them whenever their parents lost custody.

When their grandmother passed away though, the State of Florida felt the adult siblings would not be able to cope with the emotional and financial stress of caring for all of the children. So the youngest baby was adopted, and Johnny, Cristina, and Kayla were placed in the foster care system.

Once in foster care, they lived in fifteen different homes over a period of eight years. One can only imagine how damaging this must have been for the siblings. Some believe more damage is done to children in the foster system than they would experience in a family home. One of the girls vividly remembers being sexually abused while in a foster home, whereas the other does not. Many abused children repress bad memories just to survive but still suffer the awful consequences. In one of the fifteen different homes they had been placed in, Child Protective Services found Johnny, Cristina, and Kayla locked in dog cages in the backyard. My heart just bled for these kids. They'd been through so much.

I knew that the situation was bigger than we were. I chose to trust God and accept that He put these children into our lives as part of His greater plan. Although I had to frequently coax myself out of my anger, I earnestly tried to understand them, taking into account their history and the extreme trauma they'd suffered. I wanted to show them a loving family and how to look out and care for each other. I made intentional choices, choosing to love them, even when it hurt. I chose to keep trying, to keep praying, and to go on loving them even as they pushed me away. I also chose not to give up. And, most importantly, I chose to accept that adoption is forever, just as God has adopted us into His family.

How could I do that now that Johnny was gone? How could I get Cristina and Kayla through this new trauma? As we pulled into our driveway, the adrenaline of the 1,000-mile drive to get our family home safely crashed. I was overwhelmed with enormous grief combined with the overwhelming thought of how Johnny's death was going to impact Cristina and Kayla.

This was an awful time in our lives. Just losing Johnny was heartbreaking in and of itself, but the tragedy also shattered Cristina and Kayla's trust in our ability to care for them. I asked myself the same questions that anyone would in this situation: What if we hadn't gone? What if we had done something differently? How could we fix this? Those questions went unanswered though, and I began to wonder where we had gone wrong. Of course, over time, I realized that some things are simply beyond our control, but in that moment, I had to dig deep to stay strong.

When I try to find meaning in Johnny's death, it becomes clear to me that God used Johnny to bring Cristina and Kayla into our lives—there's no doubt in my mind. We had absolutely no intention of adopting more girls. Although Johnny's death marked the beginning of a very difficult time, I chose to continue following God. I also chose to acknowledge that I loved Johnny very much, that his death hurt my heart, and sadly, that his death had begun to chip away at my blind faith in God.

CHAPTER THREE

Seizures Hit Hard

Unfortunately, Johnny's death was just the beginning of the trials that we would face as a family. The next setback revolved around another of my sons, Reggie, and started out of the blue one Christmas Eve.

With all her children grown and enjoying Christmas at their own houses each year, my mother had introduced a tradition of holding a family breakfast at her house on Christmas Eve. Our family is a large one, and my mom's husband's family was just as big. There were kids everywhere, running around boisterously and bubbling with excitement. Happy little Miah, the youngest, was following Reggie around. There were lots of people at their house that day, and everyone enjoyed eating together and spending time with family, particularly with the kids. My brother Wayne was playing with the children in the backyard. He held both of their hands tightly and started to slowly spin them around until their feet lifted off the grass. First, it was Miah's turn, and then Reggie's. Being a sensory seeker, it was a game Reggie especially enjoyed.

I heard Reggie's laughter rise above the noise of the family gathering. It floated into the kitchen where I was conversing and catching up with family. The kids were having a good time and I continued chatting until I was jolted by someone yelling "Cristi!" in a panic. I rushed outside to the source of the scream, and I saw Reggie on the floor in the throes of a grand mal seizure. He was convulsing, foaming at the mouth, and every muscle in his body had grown rigid. I hurried over and kneeled next to him, turning him onto his side. My training and experience told me what this was and what I should do, but no amount of practical knowledge could have emotionally prepared me for witnessing my child experiencing his first grand mal seizure. I did my best to suppress my alarm and asked for a cushion that I could put under Reggie's head. "Call 911," I said and held Reggie on his side.

Although the ambulance and rescue workers arrived pretty quickly, the seizure had ended by the time they got there. During a crisis, I tend to freeze emotionally as my brain tries to process the information it's receiving from different angles. Although I held it together, I recognized the magnitude of what this seizure meant. I knew that it wouldn't be the only seizure that Reggie would have. In fact, it confirmed my suspicion that there was definitely something wrong with him.

The rescue workers transported Reggie to Baptist Hospital where medical professionals monitored him closely and ran a barrage of tests. The acute seizure had long passed and there was not much else they could do. The neurologist on staff that day looked at us with a mix of harsh authority and pity. "I've never seen an EEG so abnormal," he said. Here he was, a pediatric neurologist who assessed children and interpreted EEG's daily, and yet he had no idea what was going on. I'll never forget the words he said next, as they still weigh heavy on my heart. "I don't know what it is, but it's bad." I was terrified and wanted some answers. Why wasn't I getting any?

Reggie seemed to be back to his normal self soon after, laughing and playing. As for me, I just wanted to run away from this bad news and uncertainty, so I requested for him to be discharged. Normally, they might not have allowed it, but with my experience as a nurse, and it being Christmas Eve, they let us go home early rather than being stuck in the hospital on Christmas Day. Even so, Christmas for me that year, and every year after, would never be the same.

Reggie had been born completely healthy with nothing that would have given us any concern. For the first three years of his life he developed normally and hit all of his milestones, even hitting some early. First steps, first words, his development was proceeding as it should, but at three years old he started to struggle with developmental delays. At that point, Reggie had already been diagnosed with ADHD. Then he was diagnosed with dyspraxia in May of 2006. As it turned out, the diagnosis of dyspraxia wasn't significant because it's a blanket term for "difficulty controlling movement or speech." The doctors struggled to figure out exactly what was happening with Reggie. Another doctor diagnosed him with autism, which can be used as another blanket term, but autistic children typically have social difficulties that Reggie never had. He was always extremely social.

After the seizure, I was in a state of shock. The event made all of the work that I had put in trying to help Reggie's condition seem worthless. It also underscored the fact that his learning problems were far bigger than I believed and that he was much sicker than I understood. Around the same time, Miah started having difficulty maintaining the academic standard at the advanced school she was enrolled in. Thinking it just wasn't the right fit, I transferred her to a regular school. Although I didn't understand exactly what was happening with my children at the time, I made the choice to keep learning, to keep going, and to never give up. I chose to fight, constantly adjusting to our new normal. That "normal" involved life without Johnny, raising my remaining six children to the best of my ability, dealing with trauma, navigating grief, and getting to the bottom of whatever was wrong with Reggie.

Reggie and Miah were very close, and the issues surrounding Reggie hit Miah hard. She is, and always will be, my baby girl. Miah is the youngest of all of the siblings. We used to joke that she was the easiest child, but it was actually true. Even Miah's birth was "easy." I wanted my parents, her Grandpa West and Nana, to be present for her arrival. They were waiting patiently at the hospital when the doctor insisted that it would be some time before Miah would come and that they should get some air. Reluctantly, they decided to go off campus, not far, about five minutes away, and grab something to eat. Wouldn't you know it, just then, Miah decided to make her entrance, with very little pomp and circumstance, before they could get back.

Miah was also considered an easy child because family and friends alike couldn't help but compare her to Reggie. When Reggie was bouncing off the walls, Miah was quietly playing with her stuffed animals and dolls. She was always a sweet presence, smiling with a quiet confidence and trailing behind Reggie, even though that sometimes meant being in the direct line of fire (swinging golf clubs and other such shenanigans). Miah looked up to her big brother, but when asked about him, she wouldn't be shy in informing you that Reggie did not like to share. Because she had a kind and giving nature, Miah didn't understand when others did not act the same way. She rarely complained or expressed dissatisfaction, though, and loved being a part of our big family. Miah remained a beacon of light despite the drama and illness in our daily lives.

It was a blessing, after all, to have four daughters, each one different from the next. In contrast to the sweet-natured Miah, Kayla has always been a force! I love her with all of my heart, but she can be a very strong-willed individual. And, after Johnny's death, we (understandably) saw some of her more negative character traits escalating. Bundy and I were distraught at Johnny's death, but we had the life experience and backgrounds to help us cope. Kayla didn't possess the emotional tools needed to deal with such a huge loss and was just not able to make sense of the world after Johnny's death. This led to some more pronounced issues with her behavior. While Kayla had been somewhat emotionally distant before Johnny's death, afterwards, she had become almost hard-hearted. Of course, these were fairly natural responses to the additional trauma she experienced as a result of his death, especially given the extreme hardship she and her siblings had already been through in their lives.

Cristina was similar to Kayla in terms of the grief, trauma, and behavioral issues that followed in the wake of Johnny's death, but she was completely different in how she was expressing herself during that time. Cristina always loved hugs, but now, she wanted them all the time. It was about reassurance for her. I did my best to supply them, as much as I could, and watched her love on Reggie and Miah. Although Kayla wasn't as willing to be physically affectionate, Cristina kept a close eye on her, making sure to keep her within reach. Cristina wanted to make sure that her other siblings weren't going anywhere.

Cory was the solid, older brother of the group who always tried to bring joy into the chaos. He loved making people laugh and was well-liked because he was fun to be around. Cory felt his purpose in the family was to entertain the other kids. He tended to avoid difficult situations and issues, however, and began to adopt a laissez-faire approach to life. Cory eventually met a girl, moved in with her, and then disappeared from our lives for about two years. Bundy was a little disappointed but felt we had done what we could for him. Cory had become a man and was making his own choices.

Cory's disappearance really hurt me, especially when I discovered that he had been living with his biological mom for a while. I cried over it several times, wondering if he still loved me. Deep down, I was feeling sad and betrayed. After some time passed though, I gained more clarity and understood that if I were in Cory's position, I would also want a relationship with my mom. It was still hard for me, and at times I thought, *she didn't make the effort to keep him, and now that he's an adult, she wants to resurrect the relationship.* Looking back now, I feel guilty for judging her. All I really wanted was a relationship with my son (just like she did).

And our family just wouldn't be a family without Nidra. She was the first to become an adult and to move out of our home, but she always remained a part of the family. Nidra met someone and began a relationship. Some time passed, and when I saw her, she seemed different to me. So the next time we were alone I asked her about it. "I know you have something to tell me," I said. Nidra responded by letting out a deep sigh. "I'm pregnant," she'd mumbled. My mind raced back to when I was sixteen years old and pregnant. I'd experienced the extreme fear of being ill equipped to deal with a baby, sadness at the loss of my youth, anxiety about the future, and the uncertainty of not knowing what to do about any of it. My mother and grandmother had offered to pay for my abortion, and we made the decision without much thought. It had all been arranged. As I looked at Nidra in a similar spot, I had a sense of the difficulties that lay ahead of her—the challenges facing a young, single mother—and I began to understand my own mother's concern for me, and why she offered that choice (the abortion) on my behalf. I didn't remember us discussing any other options, and I never even considered that I was carrying a living child. I guess it was the selfishness of my youth. Little did I know that guilty thoughts over it would plague me for years to come.

I felt protective of Nidra and didn't want her to be burdened with the responsibility of a child before she had firmly established the course of her life. As a Christian, and having had personal experience, abortion wasn't a route that I was willing to discuss, so I went with the next obvious option. I'd recommended that she give the baby up for adoption. Nidra's determination and self-assurance were made clear when she refused to give up her baby. Because Nidra was my adopted child, though, what she said next troubled me. "I think adoption is worse than abortion." I was hurt, but when I saw the depth of her emotional attachment to her unborn child, I regretted suggesting adoption to her at all.

For Nidra, someone who had a biological mother who she felt didn't love her, suggesting that she give her baby up was the worst thing I could have said. I feel so guilty about suggesting that Nidra give her child up and still beat myself up about the emotional rift it caused between us for a time. Looking back, I am glad that Nidra had the emotional resolve to make her own decision.

My marriage to Bundy was impacted by the ups and downs our family was facing. During that time in our lives, it seemed to me that Bundy was not mindful of what was going on with the family or the issues that Reggie was struggling with. I later realized that he was just scared and confused. The two blows to our sons were swift and powerful—Johnny's death followed by Reggie's medical issues. Bundy was having a hard time dealing with it all. To me, it felt as if he had checked out emotionally and that all the difficult decisions were left to me. Many people respected Bundy as a community leader for youth, but I was frustrated by his lack of mental and emotional support in our home. Still, I did my best to remain a loving wife and tried to see his side of things.

Before long, we went from parents to grandparents. In September of 2006, Nidra had her first child, Savanna. This sweet little girl made a grand entrance into our family, arriving twelve weeks early, weighing a mere two pounds and eight ounces. A preemie, she was put on a ventilator to assist her tiny lungs and spent the beginning of her life in the neonatal intensive care unit. Nidra was a pillar of courage and resilience as Savanna struggled to flourish for the first few years of her life. We were all beside ourselves when the doctors informed us that she would need surgery on her underdeveloped little heart.

I tried to support Nidra, and be as much help as I could. Nidra was independent now, though, living on her own, and quite honestly, I was wrapped up with Cristina and Kayla's issues and Reggie's health. Happily, it all turned out well in the end, and Savanna's surgery was a success. I was so proud of Nidra and how she stayed strong during that tense and critical period. Seeing her with Savanna now, I again deeply regret suggesting that Nidra give her up.

During this same time, Reggie's medical condition worsened as I continued the attempt to tackle it head on. I decided to try herbal supplements, which led me into the expensive world of alternative medication. Each doctor has their own method of treatment. They prescribed loads of supplements, costing us thousands of dollars. I did this over and over with each new diagnosis —hyperbaric oxygen and special diets, gluten free, casein free, and so on. It was exhausting and was not producing significant results.

In 2007, Reggie started chelation therapy, and heavy metals, specifically arsenic, were emerging from his body. I investigated the possible sources of the arsenic he may have been exposed to, trying to locate any area that could have contributed to his problems. By 2008, Reggie's seizures had become uncontrollable and were increasing in frequency and intensity. I was heartbroken but continued to search for answers. I eventually took him to

New York University (NYU) Epilepsy center where they diagnosed Reggie with Lennox-Gastaut Syndrome (LGS.). I was
not satisfied with this diagnosis, angry even, knowing LGS was
just another "blanket" diagnosis. As such, I refused to accept
it and returned to our doctors in Miami to get their opinions.

By this stage, I was beyond frustrated with the medical
professionals and all of their empty promises. I had been hopeful
that I would get some answers from the NYU Epilepsy Center;
after all, they were supposed to be the best. But theirs and all
of the other diagnoses seemed useless and incorrect. Reggie's
seizures and developmental presentation were very different
from other children with the same symptoms. These doctors
were just guessing with diagnoses like autism, LGS, and mental
retardation. One even went as far as to say, "Some kids are just
mentally retarded and have seizures." What? I wanted to throw
something at him! I knew that Reggie had been born completely
normal and had been deteriorating over time. Even his IQ was
decreasing. My head spun at the many hospital visits, and I still
wasn't getting any answers.

During these challenges, my mental strength faltered but
was not defeated. There were many choices for me to make, and
I knew that strength was what was going to get Reggie and the
rest of my beautiful family through our challenges. I loved all
of my children more than anything else. So I made those choices,
one after the other. I chose to ignore the negative and indefinite
information. I chose to not believe the skepticism. I chose to
keep looking for hopeful doctors. I chose to continue to love
on Reggie and the rest of my kids and do my best to help them.
And you know what? I became more and more confident in

my choices and in my strength. The decision to go back to our Miami doctors was one of my best. They strongly disagreed with the diagnosis of Lennox-Gastaut Syndrome and continued assessing Reggie. In the end, this wrong diagnosis was what provided them with the renewed motivation to find the cause of Reggie's illness. I was not giving up on Reggie. I was not giving up on Miah. I was not giving up on Cristina or Kayla. I was not giving up on Cory or Nidra. I was not giving up on Savanna. I was not giving up on Bundy, and I sure as hell was not giving up on myself! I was choosing to take control, and I did.

CHAPTER FOUR

PTSD
Almost Ruined Us

I kept moving forward with my can-do attitude, but there were many more trials along the way. Some were medical and others were behavioral, like one of the many days when Kayla was giving us a serious run for our money.

"This man abuses me!" Kayla told the ER nurse after Bundy left the room for a soda. When he returned, Bundy was taken into a private room with two security guards. They told him what Kayla had said. His anger level returned to where it had been an hour earlier when he'd wrestled Kayla off of me. And Kayla's accusations didn't stop there. "He broke my foot because he lost his temper, and this isn't the first time he's abused me!" It suddenly struck Bundy that nobody there knew the truth; his feelings were validated by the two security guards who eyed him with suspicion. "The police will be here shortly to question you," they said. They turned their backs and closed the door, locking it behind them. Bundy was shocked, hurt, and angry, but another emotion dwarfed all of the others: his heart was aching with the sharp pain of his daughter's betrayal.

When the police arrived, Bundy was thoroughly interrogated. After answering some harsh questions about the alleged child abuse, the officers withdrew from the room. "It's a strange feeling," Bundy said, "knowing your own innocence, yet somehow feeling a sense of shame and guilt. I suppose it's the thought of these strangers—who don't know my heart and possibly don't believe me—thinking I might actually abuse my own children."

Even as Bundy sat there with his head in his hands, feeling betrayed, the ordeal was not yet over. As soon as the police left, an official from Child Protective Services entered the room to continue the interrogation. "What happened here?" More questions and more hard feelings. This event marked a pivotal change in Bundy's relationship with Kayla. He's had a really hard time trusting her again, and I think she had difficulty interacting with him as well. It was little wonder that Kayla was showing such significant signs of distress after Johnny's death, given her history.

This particular incident happened at the height of it all. In the beginning, I hadn't really realized how bad it was or how bad it was going to get. In May of 2008, I gave Kayla her first cell phone for her fourteenth birthday. I thought I was doing something nice for her, but now I'm fairly certain that this gesture was exactly how I lost control. It wasn't long after that I found explicit texts and pictures on her phone. I tried to counsel her about it, but she wasn't having any of it. In fact, Kayla rebelled and began running away from home.

The first time she ran away I was beside myself at the thought of Kayla being out there by herself. I wanted to protect her and now I couldn't find her. The first time a child runs away from home, the police actually look for them. The second time you report a runaway child, however, they're considered a chronic runaway and are simply listed as missing—the police don't even bother looking for them. When Kayla first ran away, I actually had about twenty cops and a helicopter looking for her, but after that...nothing. They won't do it again. At that point, your hands are tied; you just start calling people you know, hoping your child stays connected to some of the friends you can contact, friends who can give you some hints and clues as to their whereabouts. Luckily, this time Nidra was able to find her. She tricked Kayla into being outside at a specific time, and then Nidra and Cory aggressively removed her from the area where she was staying. Nidra was very angry with Kayla and how the situation had impacted our family. Truth be told, it saddened all of us, but, even so, I was happy to have her back safe. But that wasn't the end of it, though. To our dismay, Kayla ran away again and again. It was impossible to keep her off the streets. It became clear that I needed to get some help for Kayla. I wasn't going to give up on her. After lots of searching for an affordable teen program, I sent her to Teen Challenge Kansas City Girls Home in 2009. Teen Challenge is a fifteen-month residential discipleship program based on establishing a relationship with Jesus Christ and is geared toward positive life transformation and restoring relationships. Kayla would now be safe and off the streets. I hoped that she would also be on the way to learning how to deal with her childhood mistreatment and that the program would help her to overcome her reactive attachment issues. I breathed a sigh of relief. Feeling better about Kayla, I turned my attention toward sourcing doctors and treatment for Reggie. This relief was short lived; Kayla got kicked out of the program after only a few months for having inappropriate relationships there.

When Kayla came home after being expelled from Teen Challenge, I enrolled her in a small private school, and for a few months it seemed like she was doing well. But unfortunately, she became romantically involved with another student there, and in December, they ran away together. I was defeated and saddened. I wasn't making any headway, and all that I wanted to do was to protect her. I eventually decided that Kayla would return on her own when she was ready, and just prayed for her safety in the meantime. My strategy seemed to work. On Christmas Eve, Kayla did come back. I wasn't excited about her relationship or behavior but was glad that she had come back of her own accord.

I can remember that night clearly. I'd answered the door when I realized that Kayla was there, but she was not alone. I invited Kayla to come inside but refused to let her friend into our home. They both started causing a scene in our front yard, so I called the police. Despite only being fifteen years old, Kayla tried to convince me that *she* was a mature adult and that I simply needed to accept her decision to be with this person who was not a good influence. When she realized that I wasn't going to give in, she got angry and tried to leave again. This led to the scuffle that landed Kayla in the hospital with a broken foot.

I grabbed Kayla's arm to prevent her from leaving, but she went ballistic and began to attack me. I tried to get away, but Kayla just kept punching and kicking me. At this point, Bundy came out of the house and intervened. He grabbed Kayla, using a restraining technique that he had learned during his employment at the juvenile jail. Kayla fought and kicked back, managing to break her foot in the process.

The police eventually arrived and successfully de-escalated the situation which is when we took Kayla to the emergency room for her broken foot. Thankfully, the social worker who came to the hospital to investigate our case was familiar with Kayla and the problems we were having —she had been to our house several times. No charges were filed, and Kayla went away again to cool off for a while.

Kayla returned home again after a short time but soon ran into trouble. I continued to struggle with how to best help her until January of 2010, when she was approved for a four-month treatment program. That program was a godsend, and I really do believe it helped Kayla more than anything we'd tried before. Although there continued to be some incidents, Kayla was doing a lot better overall. I was overjoyed that her life was starting to get back on track. In fact, we were all extremely proud of her. When she graduated high school in 2011, every one of u s—Reggie, Miah, Cory, Nidra, Cristina, Bundy, and I—clapped and yelled with all the love and excitement that we could muster as she crossed the stage!

CHAPTER FIVE

Devastating Diagnosis

Throughout the trials with my other children, I was still doing my best to help Reggie. And that too, had many challenges. There is a day, however, that stands out for me as pivotal and life changing. It was one of those days that I will never forget where I was or how I felt. I'd decided to work that day because I wasn't concerned about Reggie's follow-up appointment and felt sure his tests would be normal.

During a previous hospital visit, one of the doctors noticed that Reggie walked in a way which could indicate the possibility of a genetic disorder in the ataxia family. "I would like to perform more genetic testing," she'd said. I thought she was going down another rabbit hole and doubted her assessment. I told her that it only happened during the postictal stage after a bad day of seizures. "I would like to do the tests anyway," she replied. I didn't see any harm in it, so I gave her the okay.

I didn't think we'd get any real information at the follow-up appointment, so I'd asked Bundy to take Reggie by himself. I typically attended doctor's visits and dealt with the bulk of the medical responsibilities, but I needed to be in the office that day. I was surprised when I received Bundy's call at the office. "I have the geneticist here. She wants to talk to you," he said. The doctor got on the phone, while Bundy tried to prevent a hyperactive Reggie from tearing up the doctor's office.

"The results came back on Reggie's tests. We've determined it is Dentatorubral- pallidoluysian atrophy (DRPLA)," she said. I typed the words into an internet search engine as she spelled them out for me. The geneticist went on to explain what that diagnosis meant, and my heart nearly broke in two. I began to cry as her words shattered my world into smaller and smaller pieces. My affectionate, lively little boy had DRPLA. No words can begin to express the depth of grief at hearing that my son would lose his mental ability and experience bone-rattling seizures and great pain.

As if that wasn't enough, the first thing I saw after typing in the difficult-to-pronounce, rare, degenerative disorder, were the words: *autosomal dominant*. As a nurse practitioner, I understood those words all too clearly. It meant that the disorder was given to Reggie by either Bundy or me, and that our daughter, Miah, would also need to be tested for it.

By now, there was a small gathering of other nurses, my colleagues, and friends in the office. They peeked over my shoulder reading the description silently on the computer screen. No one had to say a word; they (and I) knew the magnitude. I cried. They hugged me and allowed me to express my fear and anger. "We've got you covered," they said, organizing the cancellation of my classes and making sure that I made it home safely. Completely crushed, I greeted Bundy just as he arrived home from the appointment with Reggie. I tried to explain

DRPLA to Bundy just as the doctor did, but he couldn't seem to wrap his head around it.

Over the next few days, my mind raced around the information, considering it from every angle. The magnitude of the diagnosis hit me in waves. I knew it wasn't just Reggie who was sick—it was much bigger than I had initially thought. It became difficult to stay positive, but I chose not to give up on Reggie's treatment. I chose not to change my mindset just because I had been given a name for this illness. I chose to do rigorous, in-depth research into what I was fighting, and Bundy chose to let me lead the fight with my medical experience.

I was still processing and grieving the diagnosis when it was time to attend Reggie's annual school IEP meeting. IEP stands for Individualized Education Plan, and in a utopia, it is the plan to successfully teach special needs children. Most special needs parents will tell you that it's no utopia and often very stressful. The IEP meetings I attended for Reggie always seemed to be focused on what Reggie couldn't do. I would typically leave those meetings feeling defeated. Reggie started in a regular special education class at a regular elementary school, then was placed in a special program, and then eventually transferred to a special school for children with disabilities. I left each IEP meeting crying. My daily fight was to help Reggie improve, but these meetings were always about how badly he was doing and about lowering my expectations, zapping my hope. Now, already fragile, I had to go and face these educators once more and openly admit to having received this horrible diagnosis. I couldn't help but feel that it would be used as a justification for why he wasn't teachable, and I dreaded it.

After Reggie's diagnosis, Bundy, Miah, and I all went in for genetic testing. From a few oddities I'd noticed in Bundy's movements, I suspected that he would be positive for DRPLA, but felt certain that Miah would not be. There is a fifty percent chance of passing the disorder on to a child, and Miah hadn't experienced any of the symptoms that Reggie had. I was floored when the results of the testing came back. Bundy had sixty-two repeats and Miah had sixty-nine. They were both positive. Another crushing blow, a punch in the stomach that knocked the breath right out of me. I knew that according to what I saw out there in the medical community, there was little hope.

How was this possible? They were both so healthy. Miah was having some problems learning, but they seemed minor compared to what Reggie was experiencing. Bundy went into deep denial. He coached football, taught high school! Surely there'd been a mistake. In contrast to his denial, I chose hope. I continued thinking that maybe Bundy and Miah would never get sick. So little is known about DRPLA. Maybe there was or would be a cure.

Miah was only eight years old when I received her diagnosis. I decided not to share it with her yet, but my heart broke for her, nonetheless. Even if she never showed any symptoms, I knew it meant Miah should never have children of her own. With such a big heart, I couldn't imagine her not having a family to care for one day. There was a fifty percent chance that she would pass it on, and from what little is known, it gets worse with each new generation. I still fought the diagnosis in my mind. How could it be possible? How could Miah have a disease that would affect her balance and movement? She was already an amazing gymnast. Watching her on the balance beam was such a pleasure. So many of my hopes for her future were dashed. She was so full of life. Reggie too. The thought of them having DRPLA was gut-wrenching. It took all of my emotional strength to fight the grief. During this time, negative thoughts began creeping into my mind. I had to make the conscious decision once again to keep fighting the disorder that was threatening our family. It was a very difficult time. Reggie's seizures were so devastating and time-consuming that I didn't even have the emotional energy to process the reality of Miah's diagnosis, especially since she wasn't sick at that stage. I fervently held on to hope that Miah—like Bundy—would only be affected by the adult onset of DRPLA.

Some time passed, and in an effort to divert our minds from the gravity of our situation, we embarked on a Disney Cruise to give us some reprieve. The Make a Wish Foundation had granted Reggie this five-day cruise, and we were able to take Miah, Cristina, and Kayla with us. But, in our usual family style, even that adventure was not without its drama.

I'd heard the "ting" as the glass elevator reached our floor, and the doors opened. Our family got out and ambled over to the dining room. Miah was laughing and joking around with her sisters. We were all looking forward to a nice dinner after the exciting day we'd shared together.

Something was amiss, though. I looked around and asked, "Where's Reggie?" Panic set in as I realized that he wasn't with us. We sprinted back to the elevator, but he wasn't there either. Frantic, I stopped the first employee that I saw and told him that we'd lost our son. "Oh, don't worry, kids get lost all the time," he said calmly. "It's not a big deal."

"No, you don't understand!" I explained earnestly, "Reggie could jump off the side thinking it's a big swimming pool. It *is* a big deal!" He smiled and told me again not to worry.

"Let's just go to Guest Services. He'll be there." We, the entire gang, practically ran over to the Guest Services desk. Miah looked like she was in shock, worried about her brother and also picking up on all of the anxiety that was flowing out of me. I tried to keep an eye on the rest of the kids while I asked about Reggie.

"No, nobody's brought him yet, but don't worry…"

"You need to make an announcement!" I interrupted, "The kid doesn't understand he's on a huge boat."

"Oh, we can't make an announcement like that," he told us, "We don't want to scare the other guests."

The cruise had been so exciting for Reggie because he loved the Disney characters, the water slides, and the swimming, everything about it. He was ten years old, but also like a four-year-old who wouldn't wait in line. He would go to the front, give the person a hug, and then step in front of them. Everyone knew we were there on Make a Wish, so they tolerated his behavior with a smile. It also provided some much-needed time with Cristina and Kayla too, and we focused on bonding with them and enjoying the time together as a family.

While on the cruise, we stopped in the Bahamas and swam with the dolphins too. It was funny because swimming with the dolphins in the Bahamas was nothing like swimming with the dolphins in Florida. In Florida, the trainers controlled the dolphins. In the Bahamas, they had no control over the dolphins. They told us, "You can't control them; they'll come when they want to." It was comical because we knew better, but Reggie loved it anyhow and laughed and laughed. His laughter made all of us laugh too.

Reggie and the whole family had a really great time on the cruise; it was the seizures that were the only damper for him. At that time, Reggie was having seizures in a predictable pattern, two good days followed by one bad day. He would get really tired between seizures but could still do things, so we would take him down to the pool and hang out there or to the children's area where he could play.

That is where we eventually found him. Someone had brought him to the children's area instead of taking him to Guest Services, but he was fine, and was never in any danger. Although, I must admit, it was one of the longest half hours of my life. Still, I was thankful that he was okay and grateful for the quality time that I got to spend with my children on the cruise. In that moment, I chose to look at the positives in my life, and I chose to keep doing so even as it got increasingly more challenging.

CHAPTER SIX

Drugs, Gangs, and Human Trafficking

Staying positive took a lot of strength. I worried about all of my children in equal shares, but Cristina, the youngest of my sibling trio, went through some particular struggles that hit me at the core. I wondered how my sweet daughter could have gotten wrapped up in such evil. And how could I have let it happen?

When Cristina told me about it, she was emotionally detached, "They had this homemade branding iron that they put into a fire pit in the middle of the lot. On the emblem, there were these two symbols that stood for membership and unity. They kept turning it over and over in the flames until it was hot enough," she paused. "Then they told me to pull down my pants. I watched as they pressed that hot iron into my thigh. It made such an awful sound...like a hiss." Another pause. "And it hurt." The pain had overridden the sensation-dulling effect of the tranquilizers she had been swallowing just before the induction ceremony. The pain, although reduced, still had the effect of bringing Cristina to a stark realization: she was now a member of the infamous Crips.

As someone poured neat whiskey over the burn, Cristina looked at her blistered skin, wondering why it didn't hurt more. Whiskey, Xanax, and marijuana turned what should have been searing pain into mild discomfort. Although Cristina does suffer from anxiety attacks, the pills had not been prescribed by a doctor; there was never a shortage of illegal recreational drugs in the gang.

Cristina's struggles started when she was just fifteen, everything began falling apart after Johnny died. When she saw Reggie getting sick and having seizures, she became terrified that she would lose him too. Then her sister left. With so many people leaving her, Cristina felt isolated and lonely. So, she decided that it would be easier to just run away like her sister, and so she did. Although Cristina's behavior was similar to Kayla's, in that they both ran away from home and were both reacting to Johnny's death, Cristina's heart was more prone to depression. She is a sensitive soul and just wanted to escape all of the hardship that she'd endured.

The first time Cristina ran away it was to a nearby neighborhood, but it wasn't long before she was pulled over by the police in a traffic stop. When they ran her name, they found out she was a missing person and made the mandatory call to us. We had her back, albeit temporarily. The next time she ran away, Nidra and Bundy, who both had connections in the community, were able to put feelers out. "Hey guys, Cristina ran away, here's a picture. Tell me if you see her in the neighborhood," Bundy would say showing her picture to all of his football players.

"Hey, I saw her at a party at Tony's," or "I saw her walking down the street yesterday." With some help, we were always able to locate her. This became a pattern with Cristina running away from home on a regular basis, which had the family and me constantly on edge.

As I could not seem to get Cristina to stay put, I felt that Teen Challenge would also be the best place for her to learn the spiritual and emotional life skills that she so desperately needed. Once again, I felt confident in my decision and that I was protecting my daughter. In fact, Cristina and Kayla were at Teen Challenge treatment center in Kansas City at the same time. Cristina seemed to do really well emotionally and spiritually during the program. We felt it was the right decision to allow her to come home early after only ten months.

Looking back on our decision to send both of the girls away, I recognize that although I thought this was the right thing to do at the time, I believe now that it was a mistake: sending children away who already have attachment issues wasn't good for our relationship with them. The girls still refer to it as the "Jesus jail."

When Cristina returned home from Teen Challenge, she decided to run away again. And this time, she ended up running into some deep trouble. Because Cristina was wise to our method of tracking her down, she ran all the way down to the Florida Keys, where we were less likely to find her. Once she got there, we knew we had lost her, and Cristina knew it too. We didn't have any connections there. Just to reach the Keys from where we lived was about a forty-minute drive, and then another three hours to drive to the southernmost point.

Cristina took advantage of this and was gone for four months before we located her. She was determined not to let us win and was going to do whatever she could to not come back. It was during this time that Cristina became more heavily involved with drugs and alcohol and made the choice to join the violent street gang.

Gang life can be brutal, and even though she ran with the Crips for only a short period of time, Cristina witnessed some horrific violence. One incident in particular stands out in her memory. She was sitting in a car, in a less-than-sober state of mind, when she saw somebody getting jumped by a large crowd of people. They were ruthless as they laid into this guy, beating the crap out of him even long after he had lost consciousness. Cristina said, "It was like a colony of ants piling onto a piece of candy, swarming all over it. It was just crazy." I know how sensitive Cristina is to violence, so the fact she was able to watch the entire incident is surprising. She must have been on some pretty strong drugs to just sit and watch something like that without trying to save the person who was being attacked.

Cristina said, "I didn't care at the time." I try to justify this reaction in my mind as a part of the effect the drugs had on her personality. I do, however, think Cristina was suffering from severe depression as a result of PTSD, because she really *does* care about violence. It was almost as if she was so depressed that she was unable to generate a response to show she cared. Her frame of mind seemed to have a self-destructive aspect to it at the time. Although some of the emotional scars have since healed, to this day, there is still light scarring of the mark that was branded into her flesh.

When Cristina turned eighteen years old, she hoped to get herself together and enrolled in Job Corps. During that time, a friend there told Cristina about a job opportunity waiting tables in a restaurant. When the two followed up on this "opportunity," it turned out that there were no waitressing jobs after all. The man who was trying to recruit them was actually a pimp whose real agenda was to hustle the girls into prostitution.

It was terrible. This pimp had a lot of charisma which he used to flatter the girls and gain control over them. When Cristina realized what was going on, she declined the offer. The guy was persistent, though. He was a good looking, thirty-nine-year-old man, and Cristina was attracted to him. So when Cristina refused, he came on to her and got her to sleep with him. He made her believe that they were in love. Once he had her hooked, he started pressuring Cristina to have sex with other men, making her believe that she would be pleasing him by doing so. Cristina didn't realize that he was only using her.

While driving with this guy (who pretended to be her boyfriend), Cristina was involved in a minor accident. They fled the scene, hoping to convince the authorities that somebody had stolen their car, but the guy whose car they hit took a picture of them. Once the cops tracked them down, they searched Cristina's bag and found a stash of drugs, including marijuana, Xanax, and cocaine.

In typical drug-dealer fashion, the pimp convinced Cristina to take the rap. "You just plead guilty to the charge," he told her. "You're young, you'll be out by tomorrow. Don't worry, I'll bail you out." So, Cristina pled guilty. This man was obviously an old hand at manipulating the system, and he was right in the sense that because it was her first charge, she *did* get out the next day. Because she was eighteen and pled guilty, she was released on probation. When I heard a few months later that Cristina was being prostituted by this man, I was horrified. Worse yet, because she was an adult, there was nothing we could do, even as her parents. Kayla was the one who showed me a website with pictures of Cristina advertising herself. My heart just broke seeing those pictures. I felt so helpless and wasn't sure how to get her free. She was worth so much more. How could I make her see that?

Cristina got arrested again when police found drugs on the premises where she was staying during a sting. Because she was still on probation for the earlier drug charges, she was taken into custody. Four felony charges were now added to the two original charges, and along with that, she was also charged with prostitution. Because it was her second offense, Cristina ended up going to jail for a year. This stint finally opened Cristina's eyes to the real relationship she had with the pimp who was abusing her. After three or four months in jail, she finally realized that this man who she thought was her boyfriend was just using her and that he really didn't care about her. It was a hard lesson to learn, as she now has a criminal record. With the new charges, Cristina ended up with six felony drug charges against her name. Once again, I felt terrible about the bad turn her life had taken.

Cristina's time in jail gave her an opportunity to self-reflect, which led to a better understanding of how she was being manipulated. In that prison, she somehow gained the strength to walk away. She found her voice, too, and eventually the courage to tell her story. Cristina said, "I want you to tell my story, because I feel that people should know how God changed my life and that without God and my family, I might not be here today. I want people to know that no matter what you go through, anything is possible with God."

I was so inspired by my daughter's change of heart and her ability to move forward. I think Cristina finally understood that she fell victim to a human trafficker, and talking about her past would not only set her free, but also help other parents and children recognize that human trafficking happens in just about every city and town across the globe. Since then, she's continued to show maturity and strength. I am so very proud of Cristina and my other beautiful daughters.

CHAPTER SEVEN

Hope vs. Hopeless

It wasn't long before another of our daughters grabbed my attention, the sweet girl who never seemed to require much attention. I will never forget that day. The memory of it lingers vividly in my brain. It was a typical afternoon in the Bundukamara house. Bundy was at football practice, and I was in the kitchen making dinner for the family. Miah was lying on her bed reading for school, and Reggie was running around the house like the Tasmanian devil. I heard a small crash and sighed. I wondered what had gotten broken this time. It was always nonstop movement with Reggie. Then I heard the sound that Reggie makes right before a major seizure. It was like a quick and violent gasping noise. My heart skipped a beat, and I sprang into action to see where Reggie had fallen. But when I got to Reggie, he was fine. He was still running around the house, laughing and playing. I took a deep breath and tried to get back to what I was doing.

Was I hearing things? I couldn't shake the horrible feeling of trauma, like there was something that I needed to respond to. Was this just PTSD from all of Reggie's seizures? I turned off the stove and went back to check on Miah. I had a sinking feeling as I walked into her room, which was confirmed when I saw her seizing. I ran over and grabbed Miah, holding her close while she had her first of many violent grand mal seizures. I thought she was safe and that I had more time, but this seizure told me otherwise. How I wanted to scream! How unfair I thought it all was.

I held Miah for safety and comfort, hers and perhaps mine too. I didn't call 911. I just held on to her because I knew what it meant and how scared she must have been. I often did the same for Reggie. Then, as soon as I could, I hastily poked at my phone, calling Bundy. "Come home right now! It's an emergency!" The high school where he coached football was right down the street. Bundy pulled up with a screech, holding his breath for the bad news, not imagining that Miah was the emergency.

Although Miah had tested positive with genetic DRPLA repeats several years back, she had been symptom free. I was convinced that she wouldn't develop DRPLA in her childhood. Again, I hoped that she would be like her father and have adult onset, which has significantly less intense symptoms, a better prognosis, and a longer life span.

I got Miah into the car as Bundy was pulling up. "I can't believe it! Miah just had a grand mal seizure!" I yelled. Bundy and I were both despondent, sobbing and crying. Truth be told, this new twist completely wrecked us both. Miah now officially had childhood onset DRPLA. She stayed in the hospital for a few days, where they confirmed our worst fears.

My sweet Miah, my seemingly easy child, her life had now become anything but. Just prior to the seizure, Miah began having some problems keeping up with her classmates and was officially identified as learning disabled. I had wondered if the learning disabilities could be the DRPLA, but I didn't want to believe it to be true. In this moment, as in many others, I had to lean on my hope. Hope—what a difficult word in the midst of hardship. It evokes so many emotions in me. Sometimes the word brings me joy, peace, and positive thoughts for the future, and sometimes the word brings me to tears.

One thing is for certain: I refused hopelessness, then and now. I chose to believe God is good. I chose to believe in both conventional and alternative medicine. I chose to believe in the good of people. I chose to ask for help and to surround myself with encouraging people. I chose to continue praying for all of my children. I chose to pray for deep emotional healing for Cristina and Kayla. I chose to continue praying for healing from DRPLA. I chose to continue to research, seek out, and try various treatments for Reggie and Miah. In our family, Reggie was the most afflicted by DRPLA, and I'd always imagined that finding a treatment for him would also help Miah and Bundy. Through perseverance, prayer, and research, I would find a way to never give up.

So, research is what I threw myself into. I came across many proposed treatments for DRPLA or its symptoms. I tried them all. One was the ketogenic diet, a stringent and precise high fat and protein, low carbohydrate diet. Results have shown that the diet can reduce and even stop seizures in some children and can slow down the progression of degenerative disorders. So I put Reggie on that diet twice, each time for a year and a half. I thought it would make a difference, so I stuck to it, even though the preparation of each meal is onerous and it's not a fun diet for a kid.

In our efforts to try everything that I believed was promising, I raised $20,000 to take Reggie to Mexico in 2010 for a stem cell transplant. I felt very strongly that it would reverse the symptoms Reggie was experiencing. Many people around us believed in that treatment too and were very generous in their support. Bundy's best friend, my parents, and many other friends gave kindhearted contributions. I even started a blog and video update to provide feedback to the donors and to record Reggie's condition before and after the treatment.

When Reggie and I got back from Mexico, I thought it had worked. Reggie seemed to improve for three months but then became significantly worse. By January of 2011, Reggie had declined to the point where he was doing very little walking and was even having trouble eating. There is a lot of hope in transplant medicine, but looking back, I can see why it didn't work when targeting a genetic condition. Reggie's own stem cells were used, and yet, for the treatment to be effective, I believe there would have needed to be a healthy donor and a specific vector involved that would help to cross the blood-brain barrier. There is, however, still a lot of hope in the future of stem cell therapy. Later that year, I took Reggie off the ketogenic diet too. It wasn't helping his seizures, and he was already having challenges with eating. With everything else that was going on, I felt bad that not even Reggie's meals were tasty. Couldn't he have some joy? I decided to let Miah and Bundy eat whatever they wanted too. Things continued to decline. The following month, I recorded Reggie having five grand mal seizures in one day, and then it became a normal occurrence. Reggie's seizures were sometimes progressive, starting with little ones and progressing into a big seizure, but then on some occasions it was just—bam!—a big one. It was extremely discouraging, seeing this unfold, watching Reggie get worse, but I didn't give up hope.

Previously, I had tried Reggie on a course of hyperbaric oxygen therapy (HBOT), a therapy which involves breathing pure oxygen in a pressurized tube. It seemed to help some but was difficult to maintain financially. Then Reggie's condition declined further to the point where he was hospitalized for two weeks to address his pain, seizures, and weight loss. It was with a very heavy heart that I eventually consented to having a feeding tube inserted. I hated it for him but had no choice.

Next, in an effort to break Reggie's seizure pattern, which stubbornly held fast at two good days followed by one bad day, doctors implanted a small pacemaker-like generator in his chest wall, called a Vagus Nerve Stimulator (VNS.) The device is programmed to send regular, mild pulses of electrical energy to the brain in an attempt to control the seizures. I really hoped it would work, but unfortunately it could not break the cycle of two good days and one bad. Committed to never giving up, I still had hope.

I remember one Christmas when the pattern of seizures actually worked in Reggie's favor. Since the Christmas Eve of Reggie's first seizure, he had not had a seizure-free Christmas. This time he did! Reggie loved the excitement of Christmas and opening all of the brightly wrapped presents. I recall looking over at him that day. His face glowed with the anticipation and pleasure of tearing off heaps of bows and gift wrap. It made us all so happy that I even suggested rewrapping the gifts just so that he could do it all over again the next day. For just a fleeting moment, it was like the old days when Reggie's laughter filled our house.

But it was short-lived, as Reggie's health began to decline once more. He was doing very little walking, and I was having difficulty with his meals. After a serious hospitalization, the doctors recommended hospice for Reggie. Hospice? It angered me that those medical professionals wanted to give up on Reggie, our son, who I knew was a fighter. I would not give up then or ever! I chose rather to keep searching—to find something that would turn Reggie's health around—and the doctors' pessimism only pushed us to work harder to prove them wrong.

When Reggie was hospitalized for aspiration in November of 2012, the doctor attending him recommended a tracheotomy. I absolutely refused. I had to argue with the doctor to give Reggie a fundoplication to prevent the aspiration, rather than a continuous feed and tracheotomy. I felt his recommendation was given in arrogance. He didn't know the whole story, didn't really look at all the tests, and just decided "this is simply the next step in your disease process." I felt a tracheotomy is something that could be an extension of life but would significantly reduce his quality of life, so I insisted on a second opinion. Thankfully, the second doctor agreed with me. I often felt like it was always a fight to get what I knew would be best for Reggie.

I kept going, though. In January of the following year, doctors injected Botox into Reggie's salivary glands in an attempt to reduce the aspiration on his saliva. This seemed to have a paradoxical effect and worsened his saliva, cough, and aspiration. At this point, Reggie was mainly g-tube fed so they removed four of his six salivary glands, which significantly improved his quality of life. Even though he wasn't eating anymore, I would sometimes slip a bite of chocolate cake into his mouth. His response was always the same—a big chocolate- smeared smile.

As Reggie declined further, I dug deeper and stood firm on my belief that I would find something to make him better. The cost of Reggie's care and treatments, however, was becoming a severe strain on our family finances. Regular insurance would not cover in-home services, and because we didn't qualify for Medicaid, we received no assistance at all. In desperation, I contacted a congressman to get special consideration and eventually received help from the State of Florida with nursing care for Reggie. Finally, a win!

Despite the relief of the additional help, Reggie began experiencing extreme discomfort that made him scream for five days in a row. I was not able to get any sleep during that time until he was admitted to the hospital. The first diagnosis was thalamic storming, but later they called it dystonic attacks. Reggie's creatine phosphokinase (CPK) and liver enzymes were dangerously elevated, so the hospital once more recommended hospice. Again, I refused. Hospice was not the place for Reggie.

I strove to make sure that the doctors and I were on the same page. "No, this isn't the end of life. We're going to figure it out; we're going to walk out of here." And each time, we *did* walk out. Within a few days, Reggie was always better. They'd tell us to make our plans and arrangements, and then Reggie would walk out of the hospital on the day after they told me he would die. He defied their skepticism time and time again.

People often ask me how I do it, how I get through so much hardship and pain. Some have even insinuated that I'm a "superwoman." I can't take the credit. I merely do the best that I can. I am who I am by God's grace alone. I was a rebellious, self-seeking young woman, with little self-esteem in my younger years. I have used that rebellious spirit to give me the strength to never give up hope. Despite their DRPLA diagnoses, I always felt that Reggie, Miah, and Bundy would be okay. Despite Cristina's felony charges and the things she'd witnessed, I also believed that she, too, would be okay. And I maintain that Kayla will use her rebellious spirit just as I have used mine. I am also confident that I will continue to be proud of Cory and Nidra, who both have endless strength to use in incredible ways. And I realize that Johnny is in a better place now and that we will all see him again one day.

CHAPTER EIGHT

Reggie Addicts

Ours was a predicament, so I needed all the support I could get. That's one of the main reasons that I started what we lovingly called "Reggie Therapy." It's a process where people lay hands on vital organs and other body parts to help improve processing functions, and Reggie loved it. Over the years, hundreds of people came to help. Our regulars were called Reggie Addicts.

Reggie Therapy went on for three years, and for the first year, we did it every single day, non-stop, through the holidays. Then we decreased it to three times a week. The sessions were an hour long, and the therapy was done mostly with college student volunteers, generally in the evening. I taught a class called community service nursing, and the students were required to do service in the community. They could fulfill those requirements by coming out and trying Reggie Therapy, and then from there, people just kept coming.

Reggie sometimes had good days when he resisted lying still for an hour, and some days that were bad days when he had seizures or he threw up or had diarrhea. But good or bad days, there were always willing volunteers. We sat around Reggie with our hands joined to different parts, like a giant Twister game, and he did not move. We would scratch each other's noses and heads, and our standing joke—or only rule—was that everyone had to wear deodorant because we all got really close to each other.

The students called me Dr. B, and they would tell me what a unique experience Reggie Therapy was for them personally. Over time, they got to know each other, the process, and Reggie, and then they began to feel it. Reggie Therapy had a profound impact on the people involved. The way we did it had probably never been done before, and I'm certain that it will never be done for anyone in quite the same way ever again. These sessions became group therapy sessions for all of us, and I often tried to pinpoint exactly why Reggie had such a powerful effect on people. When we first began, Reggie could barely talk, but even so, he somehow developed relationships with people. We also frequently discussed the wide-ranging scope of drama going on in the Bundukamara household—at any given moment— and how I, being the mom, had to manage those dramas. I imagined what it must look like to these friends on the outside looking in.

These sessions varied but had the same sort of theme. Here's what a typical Reggie Therapy Session looked like.

"It's Ruth," I called out over my shoulder to Reggie, who was watching football highlights in anticipation of the day's game.

"Hey, Cristi. Hi Reggie. Getting ready for the game I see." She kissed Reggie on his forehead and slung her bag over a chair. Reggie smiled lovingly at her before turning his eyes back to the TV. He was always able to project such intense love with his eyes. I'll never quite be able to understand it, and I'm not just prejudiced as his mom either. Lots of other people said the same thing.

"Who else is coming?" Ruth asked, plopping down with a sigh opposite me at Reggie's massage table.

"Narin and Henly should be here any minute," I told her, "and Daniela, Crystal, and Frances."

"The usual suspects," joked Ruth. "Or should I say, 'the usual addicts'?"

Some people really seemed to be addicted to spending time with Reggie. They made themselves available whenever possible, many even traveling a fair distance to be part of the group. The doorbell chimed again, and I was greeted by Daniela's subtle fragrance as she leaned in to kiss my cheek. "Hi, Dr. B," she said, squeezing my shoulder before making a beeline for Reggie. Daniela, a beautiful, well-dressed, Colombian woman, clicked past me in her heels before cupping Reggie's face in her hands, kissing him three times on the forehead. "I missed you, little buddy," she cooed at him. Reggie ate it up.

I heard another knock and greeting. It was Narin and Henly. "Hi, Dr. B. Hi, Reggie, Ruth, Daniela," Henly called out, nodding at each of us in turn. His voice, a deep baritone, offset Narin's quiet, gentle tone. It often struck me how diverse a group of Reggie Addicts could be. Henly's personality displays a certain machismo, outgoing and talkative. He left no doubt of his opinion on any subject. Narin, on the other hand, had a small frame, and although he didn't talk much, was always actively participating and cared deeply for Reggie. Both men were extreme Reggie Addicts. I was initially quite surprised by Henly's love for Reggie—it didn't seem to fit his personality—but when he kept showing up, I soon realized he was definitely part of the inner circle.

Crystal and Frances arrived within seconds of each other and were the last to join today's therapy team. "Maybe a bit closer, so Reggie doesn't strain his neck," directed Ruth, addressing Henly and Daniela. They were moving the massage table to a spot nearer to the TV, so we could all watch the football game with Reggie while we completed the therapy. Crystal and Frances greeted Reggie and the rest of us as they entered the living room and joined the fold. Crystal is super sweet and is the kind of person everybody likes. She tends to listen to the rest of us babble without really offering any strong opinions. Frances is also very amiable, yet strongly opinionated and rather eccentric, an artist—outspoken and confident.

The mixed crew gathered around Reggie, taking our seats according to where each of us would be focusing on the different parts of Reggie's body. Once we had placed our hands on Reggie, we were silent, tuning in to the task at hand. Then the football game started, and I heard the excitement in the commentator's voice as Ryan Tannehill of the Miami Dolphins connected with Dustin Keller for a 22-yard touchdown. That broke the silent concentration around the table, and Daniela, frowning slightly, turned to me, and asked, "How is Miah doing, Dr. B?"

I considered her question for a moment, releasing a long sigh. "Miah is doing okay. The pattern of her seizures seems weirdly consistent though. Something triggers her to have one between 3 a.m. and 6 a.m. almost every morning." Not sure what else to say about it, I offered Daniela a weak smile. Her face tensed.

"But Dr. B, when we first started three years ago, Miah was still seizure-free, so what..." Henly nudged her with his elbow.

"It's okay. I don't mind." I looked at Daniela. "Miah had her first grand mal seizure around January of 2011, and they haven't stopped. I can't even begin to describe how sad it's been for us."

I thought about it for a moment. When Reggie had his first seizure, I was still hopeful that it wasn't a big deal. But back then, I had no idea about what we were dealing with. After Miah's first seizure, it was different. It was hard to stay hopeful because I knew *exactly* what we were dealing with.

Daniela held my eyes for a moment and then focused on where her hands rested on Reggie's abdomen. The football commentary was the only sound in the room.

"So what do they say about Miah?" Frances broke the silence in her forthright manner, clearing the tension at the same time.

"Well, we spent several days in the hospital, running an EEG and other tests on Miah. They decided that the best thing we could do was to start her on seizure medication." Frances nodded and the group succumbed to silence once more, watching the Dolphins, who were in the process of thumping the Jaguars in this preseason game.

Frances was a card. I'll never forget the first time she took part in one of our sessions. I called Ruth shortly after she'd arrived. "You better get over here, Ruth, because this one scares me." Ruth had tried to warn me in advance, describing Frances as a "sailor-cursing pothead, atheist." But Ruth liked her and so did I.

"So, if Miah is on seizure medication, how come she still has seizures every morning?" asked Henly.

"The medication helps to control the seizures," I explained. "It keeps them more or less at bay, but it's pretty powerful medicine. Unfortunately, she's had some bad side effects, so they had to lower the dose. It's a balance between controlling the seizures and keeping the side effects to a minimum."

"What kind of side effects?" asked Crystal.

"About a year after starting the medicine, Miah began hearing voices," I told Crystal whose eyes grew wide. "I was really scared she was experiencing a psychotic break, which can sometimes happen to patients with DRPLA." Crystal shook her head and asked another question, this time in a soft, shy voice.

"What were the voices saying, Dr. B?"

"Miah thought the devil was talking to her," I replied. "And that he was telling her that she was bad." A pained expression twisted Crystal's face.

"It happened a couple of times. The voices would come and go, and I finally figured out it was due to the medication." Crystal stared back down at Reggie.

The beauty of these sessions was twofold: they brought physical relief to Reggie but also had a powerful effect on many of the regular Reggie Addicts. Suddenly, Ruth, Henly, and Daniela were all cheering loudly. The Miami Dolphins seemed to be taking the game away from the Jacksonville Jaguars.

"And what about your other daughters, Dr. B? How are Cristina and Kayla?" Narin chimed in. "They are doing pretty well. They graduated from high school, and both promised they would stay home and focus on making better decisions. So far, so good."

"I bet that's been a relief," Ruth interjected with a smile.

"Yeah, it sure has." It sometimes felt as if I was reeling from crisis to crisis, so when Cristina and Kayla matured into the sensible young women they now are, it definitely released some of the pressure I was feeling.

We all watched the game for a few moments, but I could see Crystal's wheels were still turning. "So, does Miah still hear that terrible voice?"

"No, no, no," I reassured her. "It only happened a few times and then it stopped." Crystal nodded, but still looked worried. Ruth intervened.

"Tell us more about Miah's Make a Wish cruise, Cristi. I remember Reggie's cruise was to the Bahamas, but where did Miah go?" I smiled. That clever Ruth. She knew the details by heart and was only hoping to distract Crystal.

"Miah's Make a Wish cruise was a seven-day Nickelodeon cruise to the Caribbean," I told the group.

"Wow!" Crystal responded, her eyes lighting up. "Seven days on a cruise ship...that must have been fun!"

"It was so much fun! And this time, I managed not to lose any children," I added. Everyone laughed, and Ruth and I shared a glance—her tactic had worked. The group was all having fun again. "Miah really enjoyed watching the Blue Man Group every night and liked seeing her name in the LED signs before the start of the show. It was awesome to watch her face light up when she saw her name flashing across the stage."

"Tell them about the slime," Ruth said. "That slime story always gets me," she added, wrinkling up her nose in distaste. "Well, one day, they had what they call a slime-fest on board.

And Miah was chosen to participate as the main candidate. It was messy, and it had Miah's name all over it."

"I'm sorry but being covered in slime is *not* fun!" insisted Ruth. "Do you think that would be fun, Reggie?" Reggie turned his eyes to Ruth and nodded, a mischievous smile on his lips. "Ah, you would like that, wouldn't you just!" she teased.

"Oh, yeah, he would!" I called out, as something more came to mind. "The Blue Man Group actually called Miah up to the stage too and made a painting specifically for her. It was very cool." I was grateful we had been given the opportunity to spend that special time with Miah. I felt like she often got the shaft, as so much of our focus and attention had been on Reggie during her early childhood. It wasn't that we favored him, it's just that I had been consumed with finding a cure for all of the extreme difficulties he faced. Once I knew what we were fighting, I became even more determined to find a cure, one that would help not only Reggie, but Miah and Bundy, too.

We were nearing the end of our therapy session, and time was also running out for the Jacksonville Jaguars, who were trailing far behind the Dolphins. Henly's voice interrupted my thoughts. "Dr. B, if Miah only recently started showing the symptoms of DRPLA, does it mean she has a milder form of the disorder?"

"Not really, the fact that Miah experienced an early onset of symptoms means it's similar to what Reggie is dealing with. Just last year, Miah started having anxiety attacks, and her seizures became progressively worse. She just had her worst grand mal seizure to date. It was so bad that she started turning blue... it took a long time for the seizure to stop and for her to breathe properly." I shuddered even talking about it. There were murmurs around the table. Henly nodded and posed another question.

"Surely Miah would also benefit from this therapy too, if she is struggling with the same disorder?"

"We did actually try a few sessions on her. For some reason though, she didn't respond well to it...at least," I clarified, "she didn't respond as well as Reggie has." Ruth chimed in. "I think what made it more difficult for Miah to respond is that she was almost a teenage girl when we first tried it. It's different for a girl to relax when you have all these strange people putting their hands on you. It can be very claustrophobic. We also had to make sure that there were only women involved in Miah's sessions, due to the intimate nature of it all."

"Yeah, that makes sense," Henly acknowledged.

"What we also realized at that time was how very unique this experience is for all of us involved, including Reggie. I think the way Reggie responds to this therapy is what has made it so profound. He obviously enjoys these sessions, and that's what allows all of us to relax and be ourselves." We all thought about what Ruth had said for a moment, and in that space of time, I could see her words had triggered something in Frances.

"Well, as you all know, I find it easy to relax and be myself here!" stated Frances, to which we all chuckled.

"The thing is," Frances continued, "I started helping with Reggie Therapy so I could build up volunteer hours that I needed for class, but then I just kept coming back. People would ask me why I kept coming back, but they didn't know Reggie." Frances leaned forward to kiss Reggie's forehead and was rewarded with a beautiful smile. "At some point, I realized just how much I was benefiting from these sessions. I just enjoyed Reggie's company, and I wanted to be here," she continued, recognizing the important place this activity occupied in her life.

"It was then that I started actually listening when Dr. B and Ruth were talking about their spiritual journeys—their words began penetrating my soul. I found that I preferred the message of the absolute attachment we have to God rather than the bsolute nonattachment to anything and everything." Frances paused, changing tack. "Anyway, without meeting Reggie and all of you, I simply would not be the prophetic artist I have recently become." To which we all giggled a little bit more.

These sessions sometimes held a strong spiritual component, and we would discuss different aspects of our spiritual relationships. I believe that is part of what made them powerful.

"'That's beautiful, Frances," said Narin. "What are you working on at the moment?" Rumor had it that she was working on a painting of Reggie.

"Ah! Now that's a surprise." Narin looked disappointed, so Frances waggled her eyebrows at him, and we all laughed, especially Reggie. "But" she added, "you guys will be the first to see it when I'm finished painting."

"I think we can all agree on how special these therapy sessions have been for each of us," said Ruth, whose statement was followed by a round of nods. "I have sometimes picked up on the pain Reggie is feeling, and just to be sure I wasn't imagining it, I would deliberately switch hands, and even then, I would still pick up on Reggie's pain." Ruth was particularly sensitive in this area. "The point I'm trying to make," Ruth continued, "is that

I honestly believe that by helping to carry Reggie's burden, by taking on some of his pain, we are going beyond the physical realm and tapping into a spiritual dimension."

"Even if I'm not religious?" Henly asked, looking skeptical.

"Yes, for sure!" Ruth answered, giving him a warm smile. "If you step in to pick up someone else's burden, you are still fulfilling a purpose, even though you may not be aware of it." Henly considered Ruth's reply and nodded slowly.

"Yeah, I suppose that would be true," he conceded.

The clock had finally run out on the Jaguars, who finished with only four turnovers, being soundly thrashed 27-3 by the Dolphins. We knew it signaled that our session had also drawn to a close, but nobody seemed ready to go home. Narin broke the silence. "I think it's really cool that we can fulfill a purpose by easing Reggie's burden."

"I hadn't really thought about it from that angle," I said, "but it does make sense. There can be no doubt Reggie always feels better after you guys do your magic." Reggie nodded and we all laughed again. I dearly loved this special group, and my heart was content as we began moving the massage table back in place. It never ceased to amaze me how at peace with our world we Reggie Addicts were after Reggie Therapy.

CHAPTER NINE

Moving for Marijuana

The quest continued. Everyone I was acquainted with knew that I was looking for different treatments I could try in the hope of finding a cure or even just to improve the quality of Reggie's life. Some of our more liberal friends suggested I watch a special on CNN about using cannabis for the treatment of epilepsy. I tend to be more conservative, and using cannabis, personally or on my son, was not something I was open to. So these suggestions were politely ignored. But after about four or five of my friends insisted that I watch the show, I put my feelings aside and finally did.

The CNN Special documented the remarkable effects of CBD oil on children with epilepsy. I remember thinking, *Wow! This could be it!* It was exciting, but the show also highlighted the fact that the cannabis-based CBD oil they were using was only legal in Colorado. I couldn't order it to be delivered to our home in Florida. And if I went to Colorado to get some, I couldn't bring it back or I might end up facing federal trafficking charges. Ultimately, it meant that if I wanted our children to benefit from the oil, we would have to move to Colorado. I was torn initially. The oil could make a huge difference in Reggie and Miah's lives, but uprooting everything and moving to a different state felt overwhelming—an enormous decision.

So, we took a long hard look at what the move would mean for us. I knew that I wouldn't have difficulty finding work there because I have a critical needs job, and we had no reason to believe that Bundy wouldn't also find a job easily. Reggie wasn't going to school as he was in a homebound program, so I could just get a tutor to come out to him. Miah was very sociable, so I had no concerns about the transition for her. The worst part of moving to Colorado would be leaving our family, friends, and the Reggie Addicts. They were all such a big part of our lives, and we would miss them dearly.

Before watching the CNN program, I wasn't interested in the controversy swirling around medical marijuana. I didn't even realize the word marijuana was slang, derived from the racist "reefer madness" campaign.[1] When it seemed that it might actually help Reggie and Miah, however, I had to rethink my stance on the use of a substance that was illegal, at least in many states.

Rethink, I did. My whole world view changed in a matter of days. Being a conservative professional, I would have never even considered using cannabis. And yet, here I was, making a huge decision to move across the country to give cannabis to my children. I researched everything I could on the subject. I went from being completely ignorant to well-versed within a couple of days. I found a support number for a related foundation and

---

[1] Wilcox, Anna. 2014. "The Origin of the Word 'Marijuana.'" Last updated July 28, 2020. https://www.leafly.com/news/cannabis-101/where-did-the-word-marijuana-come-from-anyway-01fb.

called it many times before a woman named Heather answered. Little did I know that this woman would change my life and become one of my closest friends. She provided all of the information that I needed to help me make the decision to move to Colorado instead of waiting for what could be many years for legalization in Florida.

Notwithstanding the claims that the cannabis plant has up to seven hundred medicinal uses, it was still a difficult choice. Bundy and I both had very good jobs, strong community ties, and lived right next door to my mother and father. Our support system was solid, and we would lose a lot of that by moving to Colorado. In a very intimate prayer with God, I said, "If Reggie is ultimately going to die, I don't want to move." I feel strongly that God said, "Go."

Game on. I traveled to Colorado in October to get residency established, apply for a medical marijuana card, find housing, and look for jobs. Everything came together quickly, and we officially moved in November. The support we received from our family, friends, and the Reggie Addicts was amazing. So many people came to say goodbye, help us pack up, and get our house ready for rent. They painted our home, helped us clean, and performed minor repairs, all free of charge. I was touched and felt it was a strong confirmation that we were doing the right thing.

The treatment I wanted to try for Reggie (and Miah) is a cannabis oil called Charlotte's Web. It has a high cannabidiol (CBD) content, which has proven to be effective at controlling and sometimes even preventing seizures, and given the extremely low content of THC—the main psychoactive compound found in cannabis—it has been deemed safe for children to use. I was convinced that it would help reduce Reggie and Miah's seizures, thus improving the quality of their lives. I was not plagued by any moral conflict surrounding the use of cannabis extracts, as I had no interest in the recreational use of the plant.

Charlotte's Web CBD oil was developed by a group of brothers from Colorado—the Stanley brothers. After it's incredible success in controlling the seizures of a five-year-old girl named Charlotte, the oil, then called Hippie's Disappointment because it contained such low levels of THC, was renamed Charlotte's Web in honor of its first pediatric patient.

Not long after that, a related not-for-profit organization called *The Realm of Caring Foundation*, was started by Heather Jackson. Her son, Zaki, was the second of the pediatric success stories using the oil. The mission of the foundation was to further the research, education, and advocacy of cannabis oil as a medicinal treatment. I initially connected with Heather when I called the foundation. Heather was a huge support to us during our relocation to Colorado. I sent Heather a video of Reggie and Miah before we moved, and she said that she fell in love with them even before she met them, as if they were her own children.

I began to grow an even bigger network in our new home base too. I met many people who had left jobs and families behind, moving to Colorado to get treatment for their children. While some had moved their entire families, others were split, paying rent and raising children in two states. The cannabis refugees (as we called ourselves) consisted of people from all walks of life, varying religious and political backgrounds, but all just people who would do anything to help their children and give them a chance at a better life.

For most of us, there was a lot that we gave up with our relocations. My husband was one who certainly felt the sacrifice. Bundy had a lot of connections in our South Florida community. I remember the party I arranged for him shortly before we moved. Forty-five was his football number, so I wanted to have a big party on his forty-fifth birthday, celebrating his life and the positive influence he's had on other people. Ruth and I spent a year planning it. Bundy's friends in Maryland even went to their college and begged for his old jersey so we could display it that night. The party was awesome and very well attended. We had all the coaches he worked with, men from the church, students he had taught and coached, and even his best friends from third grade at that party. Bundy said that it made him feel greatly respected and loved. He had been sent off on a high note.

Our other children were impacted too. During the time we were making our move, Cristina was in the Keys finishing up her probation. I couldn't help but worry about my daughter because the Keys are known as a party place and it's hard to get your life together when everyone around you is partying. But I had to admit that Cristina was definitely in a better personal space. She had a full-time job and was able to pay for a little apartment. Although she still drank a lot, she was being tested for drugs regularly, so we at least knew she was living drug-free. I still was worried about leaving her. But, lucky for me, shortly after Cristina ended her probation, she left the Keys to join us in Colorado permanently.

Cory also moved and started working for the Stanley brothers, producing Charlotte's Web. In March of that next year, our family was featured in *People* magazine. The article talked about our success with the oil. And it was going well, but toward the end of April, Reggie was hospitalized and spent some time in the ICU. Miah's seizures also began to get worse, and although I still hoped the CBD oil treatment would be effective in controlling them, it didn't seem to be the miracle that I had hoped it would be.

We bought a new house in Colorado but had difficulties with the other home we'd been renting. The renter asked us to leave even though the new house was not ready for us to move into. Reggie was sick, and he was in and out of the hospital during that difficult period, so I was worried about moving him too much. Reggie's nurse at the time was kind enough to allow us to move into her living room until the improvements to our new home were completed. It is kind of crazy to think back on it—a family of an ill, severely disabled, wheelchair-bound son, residing in the living room of his nurse for almost a month. But we had a safe place to stay with a nurse on site. That's all that we needed at the time, and it served us well.

After that, things started to get a bit worse for Reggie, and he was hospitalized again for pain. Nothing was found on the CT scan, so he was discharged. The pain got worse though, so I took him back to the hospital a week later. There they discovered that the previous doctor had missed a fractured femur on the earlier scan. The fracture had disintegrated into a complete break, which was devastating as hip fractures can be extremely debilitating.

Reggie needed hip surgery. Because Reggie is highly sensitive to anesthesia, surgeries are always really hard on him. And even after the surgery, Reggie experienced various complications involving his rehabilitation. The worst of it was that Reggie's back curved into the shape of a C as the muscles of his spine contracted. This greatly impacted him, and his quality of life forever changed, and not for the better, which was especially sobering because he was still so young.

My search and treatments continued. Reggie had a PICC line inserted, so I could intravenously administer antibiotics at home. I also drove him to Denver bimonthly for an entire year so Reggie could receive IVIG treatment, which I was later able to change to subcutaneous IG (SCIG) treatment at home. Next, after Reggie was admitted to the ICU several times for pain, the movement-disorder specialist and neurologist there concluded that Reggie was having severe dystonia attacks. They recommended Deep Brain Stimulator surgery, which had to be done under intraoperative MRI, which was only available at Cook Children's Hospital in Dallas-Fort Worth, Texas. I felt that it might be the solution that I had hoped for, so I packed up the family and made the twelve-hour journey to Texas.

However, similar to many of the previous treatments, the results were not at all what I expected. Reggie's seizures were reduced from three to six seizures every three days to only a couple per month, which was good but strange, as there is no medical reason why the DBS should have any effect on the seizures. The DBS, however, had no effect at all on his dystonia, which was our reason for scheduling the surgery in the first place. I was crushed! I didn't know where to turn. What was next? Fighting off overwhelming anxiety, only my love for Reggie and the drive to never give up kept me from falling into hopeless depression.

I held on tightly while on the roller-coaster ride of joyous hope and devastating disappointment. I chose to believe that Reggie would get better and that his healing was in God's plan. At the same time, a major rainstorm severely damaged the roof of our home and caused the entire structure to slip two feet down the hill. It was not covered by home insurance and cost us thirty thousand dollars. It was the last thing we needed and seemed an unusually cruel blow after all that we'd been experiencing with Reggie. Still, we did not give in to defeat. This was our life, and there was still hope. We chose to endure, love, and find joy.

And I did find joy even during those dark spots, and more often than not, Miah was the source of that joy. You see, Miah's transition to Colorado had actually been a great thing. With her friendly nature, she had no trouble making friends, which was illustrated by the full house at her Sweet Sixteen Party. She had a blast, and I was happy, as her mom, to be able to make it so special for her. It was great to see her laughing and dancing with all of her new friends, twirling around between the pink and purple streamers and strings of lights that paled in comparison to the light in her eyes. We'd hired a DJ, and Miah kept heading to his booth to request her favorites. There was even a little stage at the front of the event hall, and she loved hopping up there to show off her moves. The music was blasting all around us, and Miah's smile filled the room. She was very well connected, and everyone just adored her. It was one of the best parties ever! Everyone dressed up to the nines, and there were strobe lights and sparkles flying around the room. Probably the biggest hit of all was the awesome Candy Bar! We had Hershey's and M&Ms and peanut butter cups and licorice and gummy bears! Miah was grabbing the gummy bears by the handfuls and adored all of the attention and love she received that night. Being Reggie's little sister sometimes wasn't the easiest job, so it was awesome to let her be the center of attention for once.

For Bundy and me, the move to Colorado was a lot more complex. We were forced to make significant adjustments in our work lives and from a cultural perspective as well. I was born and raised in Miami, so the cultural change was a shock. People in Colorado are more reserved and not as sociable, whereas in Miami people greet with a kiss and touch each other when they speak. It took us three years to make friends outside the initial community of cannabis refugees, it was a difficult transition.

Because of the high demand in my professional field, I had a job when I arrived. For Bundy, it was different. We thought it would be easy for him to do the same because Bundy gets along so well with people; we thought that he would apply and have his choice of jobs. But that was not the case at all, and it was a big blow to his self-esteem. It turns out that there was not a need for the cool football coach-type teachers in Colorado. I was also concerned about him physically because there was increasing evidence of his DRPLA with mild ataxia and dementia.

It would be against the law to fire someone for displaying neurological symptoms, but when people interviewing you don't know what the symptoms are, they're not willing to risk finding out. Bundy is friendly and had all the qualifications, but didn't get any positive feedback from the several districts where he applied. When we shared this fact with his first neurologist, he said, "You really need to go on disability." And he did, which was a major turning point for Bundy. He realized that he didn't have what he had in Miami. There, he was a pillar in the community and had earned their respect. Here, he didn't get the chance. Sometimes I feel guilty about that.

Bundy had to find purpose again, and being an effective father was a big part of it. In Florida, he was working and coaching all the time, so he wasn't able to spend much time at home. Now, to make up for that, he spent all day with Reggie and his nurse. He also drove Miah to school and picked her up. Bundy felt he had been given an opportunity to be a better father than he had been previously. When something is taken away, something else always shows up in its place, and you keep moving forward in a new way.

CHAPTER TEN

Love Brings the Family Together

O ur children weren't the only ones that Bundy gave back to. His brother and many others were also the recipients of his kindness. In fact, he went as far as to give his brother a kidney (as if we didn't have enough going on already).

While nurses, family, and friends were caring for Reggie and Miah, I hunkered down in a post-surgical waiting room on the other side of the country to hear word on Bundy, my back pressed up against the hard chair. The surgeon had told me it was a simple procedure and shouldn't take longer than an hour. Five hours had passed, and there was still no word. While I sat waiting, desperate to hear some news about my husband, I recalled how the transplant team at the University of Maryland had initially denied Bundy's application to donate the kidney to his only brother, Adam.

Soon after we'd moved to Colorado, he was finally approved. Bundy really wanted to do it even though he and Adam weren't very close at the time. The initial denial was due to Bundy's

DRPLA diagnosis. Although ethical reasons were cited, I fought for Bundy to be able to give a kidney to his brother. We obtained letters from various doctors and agreed to sign additional legal documents, so when no other donors became available, the transplant team agreed to the operation.

It's possible I feel so strongly about my husband's generosity of spirit because that is what makes him so incredibly different from most people. When the surgeon finally came into the waiting room, I had a laugh. He told me that Bundy was so muscular that it had taken five hours of aggressive surgery to remove his kidney. "Bundy's doing well, though, and the kidney has been successfully transplanted inside of Adam's body, where it is hard at work already," the doctor said. I was relieved.

Bundy knew that his brother could die if he didn't get a kidney, so he didn't hesitate, choosing to help him because he could. Maybe he knew, deep down inside, that even though he was doing everything possible to help Reggie, his son was becoming increasingly ill. Bundy was, however, able to help his brother. So he did it for both of them, to make a positive difference in a family member's life.

Bundy's kidney was not rejected by Adam's body, but sadly, about a year later, Adam was diagnosed with the same post-transplant cancer that their mother had died from twenty-five years earlier. Everyone had known the risks beforehand, but there had been no other option for Adam. Although we'd all hoped for the best, that was not enough. I still felt extremely proud of Bundy for his absolute willingness to help, even at his own expense—a true expression of love.

I've been asked why Bundy would choose to sacrifice so much for his brother while going through extreme stress of his own. We always have a choice. I believe that life is about choices, and at some point, you realize that choosing to sacrifice your time, energy, or money is also choosing to move forward and grow in strength. We are all ordinary people and can be given extraordinary strength, hope, and love when we need it.

Relationships are, and always have been, a priority for both of us—relationships with our children, our friends, our family, and just people who needed us for a moment, a day, a month, or a year. Some of those relationships were hard, but they were always strong and forged out of love. My children have always been the deepest relationships of all, and I'm excited to say that all of my adult children eventually moved to Colorado.

Cory was the first of my children to join us when he got an opportunity to work in Colorado. Shortly after, Kayla came too. Her first stint in Colorado was short-lived though, because she met and became involved with a man in the military and moved in with him. When Kayla got pregnant, they got married and moved back to Florida together. They lived with his family in Miami, which is where Kayla gave birth to Alexandra, a lively baby girl. Sadly, however, their marriage became increasingly toxic. Even though there were clear signs that the relationship wasn't going to work out, Kayla really *wanted* it to work, so she chose to stay with him. It wasn't until Kayla finally realized it was doomed that she moved back to Colorado with Alexandra. Becoming a single mother forced Kayla to mature, and for the first time, I felt like she was going to be okay. I was proud of her.

Soon after that, Cristina completed her probation in the Keys and also moved to Colorado. Once here, she graduated from a Certified Nurse Assistant program, got a full-time job, and was attending church regularly. Cristina was doing so well, in fact, that I was somewhat surprised when she announced that she was pregnant too. Cristina and the father had not developed a meaningful relationship, so she also became a single mother to a beautiful baby girl. I was proud of my daughters, the two sisters, but like any caring mother, I wanted more for them.

Meanwhile, Nidra bought a house in Florida and had settled nicely into family life. Her daughter, Savanna, was already ten years old, and her son was eight. I believe the small rift in our relationship that developed from my suggestion of adoption was put behind us. Nidra taught me that conception is never a mistake, and I am grateful to her for showing such wisdom and maturity. She really is a great mom, and as a mother, I am awed and moved by her. Like the others, Nidra eventually moved to Colorado as well, the last child to join us. I was so very happy to have all of my dear children back together in one state.

Busy and often overwhelmed as a family, I was able to apply for resources and get some nursing assistance to help us with Reggie, and sometimes Miah too. Unfortunately, Miah's seizures continued to worsen. There was one really bad one where she lost her balance and fell forward onto her face. Miah broke her front teeth, busted her lip, and ended up with a swollen eye. She looked like she had been in a fight, and honestly, she was. It was a fight with DRPLA. Shortly after the incident, she was hospitalized for the increased number of seizures she was experiencing. Her EEG reading recorded over three hundred seizures in a timespan of fifteen hours. It was heart-wrenchingly difficult for me and the entire family to witness the steady decline of both Reggie and Miah.

And they were not the only ones. Tragedy struck once again when Bundy's brother got sick and was hospitalized with pneumonia. In the ICU, Adam went into cardiac arrest. Not long after, I received a text from their sister telling me that Adam was dead. Knowing that Bundy would be devastated, I rushed home so that I could try to soften the blow. I didn't want him to hear it from anyone else, but when I walked in the door he was already on the line with his sister, crying. I felt terrible for their family (and ours). Bundy was not only grieving the loss of his brother, but he was also grieving that the gift of his kidney did not actually save Adam's life. Little did I know that this was just the beginning of our grief process and that we would soon be grieving another of our beloved family members, another one of the children we loved more than anything else in the world.

CHAPTER ELEVEN

Unbelievable Pain

My son Reggie was having a bad day. I was concerned but not worried because he'd had days like this before. I watched his chest rise and fall, trying to decide whether to attach the oxygen or not. I determined that he seemed okay for now. I remembered that we had people coming over today for "Reggie Therapy," which we had picked up again after moving to Colorado. It was amazing in that it once again helped the participants as much as it soothed Reggie. Reggie always felt better after the hands-on therapy and seeing the friends and family who came to be a part of it.

I stroked Reggie's hair, noticing that his breathing had become labored again. Kneeling next to him, I slipped the oxygen mask over his mouth and nose and slowly turned the valve. I stayed in that position, praying and holding his hand. My baby, the seventeen-year-old boy whom I loved so much. I winced seeing his discomfort and contemplated taking him to the hospital. "Wait and see," I told myself. It was almost time for Reggie Therapy; that would make him feel better.

My mind drifted back to the day that my husband, Bundy, and I became parents. I remembered what it was like to see Reggie for the first time as a newborn. The love I felt for him that day (and every day since) was astounding. I recalled his first words, and those early, tentative, wobbly steps. I pictured him as a toddler, full of boundless energy, racing around the house and climbing over everything. Then the precocious, active brother pushing his little sister around the yard on her bicycle.

My reverie was interrupted when one of Reggie's nurses entered the room, bringing me back to the present. The pulse ox had slipped off and it was alarming, but he was fine. He seemed to be just fine. Once again, I thought about taking him to the ER, you know, just in case. But I couldn't figure out the cause of the problem (no fever or obvious signs), so I talked myself out of it once more.

Reggie had become infamous for his ability to bounce back, and I assumed that he would bounce back from this one. He had even earned the nickname, "The Rubber Band Man." I considered all the medical equipment in the house to treat Reggie, the full-time nursing staff to attend to him, as well as the fact that I'm a nurse. Maybe I was overreacting. But maybe I wasn't.

Reggie started to look better, and I felt relieved. His breathing evened out, and his vital signs were strong. I guess I had been overly anxious after all. I decided to go about my day but kept Reggie near me, just in case. I was on high alert for any signs of change in his state. As a nurse, I am trained to recognize an emergency and felt confident that I could spot one that was oncoming. I had made that same call several times in the past, like when Reggie had pneumonia and another time when he was overcome with severe pain. In both cases I drove him to the ER.

Reggie's current condition didn't appear to be an emergency to me, but I still couldn't shake my uncertainty regarding whether to take him to the hospital.

I glanced at the tiles on the floor as if they had the answer, pondering his previous close calls. Reggie was in moderate pain most of the time, so pain wasn't new to him, but its constant presence further complicated the ability to diagnose his fluctuations. I recalled the time when I took him into the hospital, and a CT scan revealed the fractured femur. I was frustrated that it had been missed by the previous doctor, because I knew something was off then, just like I sensed that perhaps something was off now too. I just couldn't put my finger on it. Truth be told, I'd been through a lot with Reggie. He experienced various complications throughout his illness.

I looked over at him for what seemed like the hundredth time that day, hoping for one of his reassuring smiles, smiles which had become all too rare. I would always sit at the edge of his bed after he had surgery, fervently praying and waiting for him to wake up. When he opened his eyes and saw us sitting there, his sunny smile always filled me with hope. Reggie's breathing remained stable, so I removed the oxygen mask and kissed him on the forehead.

My poor Reggie. He had undergone a lot over the past few years. Each new therapy or course of medicine instilled renewed optimism in me, raising my hope that this would be the one to transform Reggie's life. If not to heal him completely, to at least improve his quality of living. But my hope was destroyed time and time again when I realized that there was absolutely no improvement. I had begun to feel overwhelmed, as if there was nothing that I could do to change things. I was grasping for optimism at every turn, frantically wanting to believe in a miracle.

I felt like I was holding my breath while fighting off negative thoughts. All I could do was rely on medical technology to make Reggie better. I had chosen to never give up. I decided that in the worst-case scenario, if nothing helped, the accumulated information could at least be used to help research this disorder. A friend had told me that I was wasting my time and energy. In response, I posted the following on Facebook:

Some may think that my fight against this disorder is futile, that I'm prolonging the inevitable and causing suffering. I can assure you, I'm not in denial, and that I understand the limitations. I can also assure you that quality of life is my goal, and that we are not afraid of death. I know without a shadow of a doubt that our relationship is eternal in Heaven. I also know that God could provide a miracle, and I will continue to pray that way.

It was at that moment that I chose to think positively. I waited for that miracle. Some days it was a battle of the mind. On those days, I willfully chose to go through life's motions. My heart hurt and I was scared, but I chose not to let it affect my actions. When I felt like I wanted to give up, Reggie would have a good day and smile at me. In those moments, my heart soared, and my determination to fight was strengthened.

Noticing that it was almost three p.m., I moved Reggie to his room in preparation for the therapy session. The sound of laughter and youthful chatter made me turn my head toward the front door. The Reggie Addicts, as we still affectionately called them, had arrived to give Reggie his therapy. Trooping into Reggie's room, they brought energy, warm greetings, and hugs. The delight on Reggie's face was the highlight of my day. I had seen that same joy many times before, during horseback riding, on the Disney Cruise, on water slides, on roller coasters, and during bike races.

I could tell that today's therapy made Reggie feel better, and after everyone had left, I tested his vital signs once more. They were perfect. He was relaxed and his breathing was even. My anxiety had lessened too, and I felt much better about my decision not to take him to the hospital.

After saying goodbye to the day nurse at six o'clock, I returned to Reggie and saw that he was struggling with his breathing again. I fitted the oxygen mask to his face and watched him closely. Once more, I wrestled with the decision whether to take him to the hospital, only now things had changed. Oxygen couldn't be administered in my car, so if I decided to move him, I would have to call rescue to take him.

I kept an eye on his breathing. He seemed fine again. I called out to Bundy, who was playing games on the PlayStation. "What should we do," I asked. Bundy said that he believed that I was the one best equipped to make the decision. Ugh! The choice was back to me. My anxiety at its peak, I screamed, "Well, you're no help at all!" My response was a bit harsh, I know, but I was struggling and just wanted someone to help me decide, one way or the other.

I paced up and down next to Reggie's bed. Yes? No? My mind was in turmoil over what to do. I still did not feel that it was an emergency, but I couldn't deny that Reggie was having a hard time breathing. Finally, I pulled the trigger and made the decision to call 911. At that same moment, my phone chirped notifying me of a message that I'd received. I was surprised to see that it was from my friend, Heather. "I'm coming over to see you," it said. It was almost ten p.m. Heather runs her foundation and takes care of her own special needs child, so it was odd that she would come over so late. I called her and explained the situation. She encouraged me to call 911 but insisted that she was coming over anyway. Heather said she'd been getting ready for bed when God told her to go to my house.

Without further hesitation, I called 911. Bundy went outside to direct the emergency responders. It was getting worse. Reggie began to hyperventilate. I wanted to test the level of oxygen in his blood. Trembling, I couldn't get the oximeter to work properly. The rescue workers arrived and helped as I was becoming increasingly anxious. Heather got there just as they attached their machine to Reggie. I realized at that moment just how serious his condition was. Knowing the responders were in a better frame of mind than me to save my son, I left the room and prayed with all my might. I didn't think about or wait for God's answer. I just repeated…*oh God, please…* and held my breath.

What seemed like agonizing hours passed until a rescue worker came in. "I'm so sorry. There's nothing more we can do," he said. Nothing more you can do? I froze, and a pain shot through my chest. This isn't happening. They asked if I would consent to calling an end to their treatment of Reggie. No, no, no. I refused, unwilling and unable to give my consent, so they continued trying to resuscitate him.

But try as they may and pray as I might, Reggie was dead. Nothing will ever erase that moment or pain from my mind. He'd died suddenly, against my will and my firm belief that he would live to see his eighteenth birthday and that I would find a cure. It made me feel inadequate as a mother and really, really angry. How could I lose Reggie? Hadn't I already lost enough?

Still, I was glad that Reggie didn't suffer in those final moments, and that he died on his own terms, peacefully, quickly, and without having to experience the extreme pain he so often endured. I can't tell you how terrible it was to see my son's lifeless body. The police and rescue workers wouldn't let me touch him before the coroner arrived, hours later. I just wanted to hug him, but couldn't, so I sat slumped in an armchair in the corner, crying, numb, and defeated.

If only I'd known, but none of us were prepared for that fateful day. I had no idea what to do next and was so relieved that Heather was there. God knew I needed her and put an urgent panic in her heart so that she would visit me that night. Cristina, Kayla, and my brother Wayne were there too. We all cried and, at first, couldn't fully comprehend what had just happened to our family.

It began to sink in quickly though and there were calls to be made. My strong daughters pitched in, taking over for me when I couldn't. I just couldn't think. I just couldn't talk. I just couldn't. Cristina called Nidra while Kayla called other family members. Cory came over, too, before they took Reggie away. Nidra remained on the phone with us the entire time and we were all present together in grief. All except Miah, who was asleep in her room. I chose not to wake her because I didn't want her to see Reggie's body and also because I didn't have the emotional strength to care for anyone else. It was a night without sleep. A night full of sadness. A night where I clung to my family. In the morning, when Miah awoke, Bundy and I told her together. Her tears were salt in our wounds.

Thank God for Heather. She took emotional control of the house, coordinating police and rescue workers. She also ensured my greatest, pre-planned wish was accomplished—donating Reggie's brain to the Harvard Brain Bank for research. Heather even called the Harvard Brain Tissue Resource Center after midnight when the rescue workers weren't sure of the process. She not only reached them, but she also completed all of the paperwork and coordinated a pathologist from Denver to come to the Colorado Springs Coroner's Office to remove Reggie's brain. Just like his daddy, Reggie was able to give an expression of love through organ donation. As for me, my expression of love was letting go. I could not wish Reggie back to the daily pain he experienced. I knew that he was now free.

A few days later, we held a memorial service for Reggie, where we all came together in our grief. Everyone wore Spider-Man attire in Reggie's honor, and the room was filled with joy and color. I chose not to speak at the memorial service, as I just wasn't sure that I could. I wanted to stay strong for my husband and children. Bundy spoke about John 13:7 explaining that while we may not yet understand God's plan, we would at some stage. "Reggie was a fighter," he said, "who taught me many things. Most of all, he taught me to be like Job, who never turned away from God."

My little Miah spoke too. "I will miss Reggie so much!" she said. Cory followed her saying, "Reggie was always on the go, moving around, except when he made us all sit down about a million times to watch Spider-Man." Everyone chuckled. "Reggie was the center of the family, making us all laugh." Kayla went next, "I met an angel when I was only nine years old. Reggie was the meaning of love and had a following of people around the world." Then, Cristina read a poem and pointed out that Reggie's memorial service fell on what would have been Johnny's twenty-fifth birthday. "I can picture them hanging out together in Heaven," she said. Finally, Nidra encouraged us with by quoting from Reggie's favorite Spider-Man movie, "Whatever life holds in store for me, I will never forget these words: with great power comes great responsibility. This is my gift, this is my curse, who am I?" Reggie always had the power to bring people together, even in death.

And Reggie liked a good song too, so we gave him his fill. We sang "Your Love O Lord," followed by "Our God is An Awesome God," and "Cry Out to Jesus," and then finished with "Big Big House," all of which were Reggie's favorites. Funny how everyone left the memorial service feeling uplifted and full of joy. Reggie's influence again. Heather described it as "grief and praise."

And it didn't stop there. The celebration of Reggie's life continued in Florida a few months later, where Frances, one of the Reggie Addicts, created a portrait of Reggie for everyone to sign. We laughed, cried, and praised God for blessing us with Reggie, thanking Him for the seventeen years of love we shared with this beautiful child. His sudden death left a ragged, gaping hole in all of our hearts. I had now lost two sons and was afraid that I would also lose Miah and Bundy. Still, I kept getting up every day, doing my best, and continued to live in hope.

CHAPTER TWELVE

With Great Power Comes Great Responsibility

Reggie loved Spider-Man, and the quote "With great power comes great responsibility" is one that we all associate with Reggie. I often feel like those words are a message from him. You see, they apply to my life and experience with him. As I continue to grieve the loss of my children, I use that pain to help others on their journey of mental strength. It is my responsibility, but at the same time, it is also my gift. Grief is so complex and varies for everyone. As I often tell those who are suffering, journaling is a way to process grief and a way to heal. When Reggie died, I wrote him a letter to express all those things that I wanted to say and all those things that I was feeling.

> To my dear son Reggie,
> Words cannot express how much I love you. A flood of feelings come over me when I try to describe your personality and what you have meant to me. As I look at pictures from your early childhood, I remember my ignorant feelings of blissfulness. I remember truly believing the scripture that says, "Train up a child in the way

he should go, and when he is old, he will not depart from it" (Proverbs 22 King James Version). I believed that if I followed God's law and was a good parent, God would protect you and you would grow up to be a healthy man of God. As I lifted you up in covenant Baptism, in the deepest recesses of my heart I gave you to the Lord, truly believing He had great things in store for you. Honestly, if I knew your years would be numbered to seventeen, I would not have been so willingly submissive to God. As I look at your pictures from the age of five through twelve years old, I can't help but smile. You were a precocious boy with lots of energy and lots of love. We did so many fun things—horseback riding, swimming with the dolphins, riding roller coasters, endless hours in the pool, repetitive trips down the water slide, bike racing, vacations, cruises, even missionary work. I remember you counting to ten in Spanish while swimming with the street children in Mexico. You had a really good life, and I'm glad that I spoiled you. As I look at pictures from the last five years, I see the progression of DRPLA taking my boy—ever so slowly, but way too fast. There is a heavy, crushing weight on my chest. I desperately want to say I am so sorry, Reggie. I did my best, but my best wasn't good enough. I'm sorry for the precious, wasted time and energy we spent on aggressive treatments that didn't work. I didn't know and I had to try. I'm sorry that I am not smart enough to find a cure. I'm sorry that it became increasingly more difficult for me to hold you. It hurt my heart so much when my touch no longer soothed you. I am sorry I struggled to maintain my hope. I am sorry I spent so much time and energy being angry with God. I'm sorry I didn't take you to the emergency room that fateful day. I'm sorry I continued believing that you would be healed, and never said goodbye. As I grieve and wrestle with God over your death, I have to remind myself daily that you are happier now than any passing happiness I could ever have provided. If I truly believe what I say I believe, then I should be happy for you and look forward to eternity in Heaven with you, but my heart aches. If I believe what I say I believe, then I have nothing to be sorry about, and I should be able to rest in God's perfect plan. I ask God, "Why do I have to feel so much pain? Why is there such a disconnect with the heavenly realms?" I lie down at night and ask God to allow me to dream of the heavens and to see your happiness, but I wake with just my faith. Reggie Josiah Bundukamara, I love and miss you so much!

All my love, Mom

How did I come to terms with this unbelievable loss? I had a process. I committed to reading my final letter to Reggie to all the people who were interested in his story—to every person willing to listen. The more I read this letter, the more real my son's death felt. People talk of "acceptance" and "closure" when grieving the loss of a loved one, but I feel that is the wrong terminology. Although I do accept that Reggie is no longer here with me physically, the goal I hope to attain goes beyond closure in the usual sense. I am looking for more than an emotional conclusion to a difficult life event. I don't want to simply relegate Reggie to memory. What I hope to achieve is a better understanding of life and death, and how they relate to eternity. Specifically, I want to focus on how I can live for eternity while still fulfilling my purpose here by helping people now. And I am still focusing on that today.

After Reggie passed away, I tried to figure out how to move forward knowing that both Miah and Bundy were still struggling with DRPLA. I fought very hard for Reggie and really believed that I could win, but I lost anyway. I realized that without a miracle, it was highly unlikely that I would win for Miah and Bundy either. So, I decided to fight, *believing that I could win.* I decided, instead, to keep investigating every new medication and therapy, but at the same time, to make everyday matter and to continue living life for eternity.

The night that Reggie died, I felt a range of emotions. Shock was followed by anger and sadness. How could this happen? Once I began to process the reality of it, those emotions gave way to a deep, unimaginable, and indescribable pain. I was struggling and chose to wrestle with God in a very personal way. I believe God recognizes the intentions of our hearts and must have understood the sincerity of my plea when I asked why Reggie died despite my prayers for his healing. God has spoken to my heart twice so far in this regard.

The first time occurred while I was praying, sobbing, and begging for Reggie's forgiveness. I somehow felt that Reggie knew all of my sins and mistakes. In the midst of my tears, God gently said to me, "Reggie saw you like any young child looks to his mother—he saw you as perfectly loving to him. Reggie is not omnipresent nor omniscient, only I know the details of your heart."

The second time, I was crying and praying yet again. I questioned God about those verses in the Bible that suggest you can ask God for anything and you will receive what you asked for. I'd pleaded with God for years to heal Reggie, and I wanted to know why my request was not answered. I sat in silence for a few moments when I heard a voice. Although it was not the response that I sought from God, I was given an even greater gift. In that moment, in that quiet space, I heard Reggie say to me. "Mom, you think you are so smart, but you have *no idea*. I'm okay; Dad and Miah will be okay. And you're okay."

Those were not words I would have said to myself—the words, the tone, the inflections were all clearly Reggie. He and I had communicated with body language and nonverbal cues for years, so I knew it was him. It was only a moment in time, and there are no words to completely describe Reggie or the heavenly realm, but I can say with certainty that Reggie has a supernatural contentment. In that moment, I experienced a peace that surpasses all understanding. I was calmed and pacified, and still cling to that moment when I suffer recalling the losses I've experienced here on Earth.

Reggie served his purpose here in this world, but I am still fulfilling mine. I can't let my experiences and losses be in vain. I didn't even realize it at first, but over the last ten years, I was slowly developing what is now known as the Mentally STRONG Method to help myself handle the immense stress I was experiencing. When I saw it working, I knew that I had to share it with others. If I'm capable of making this world a better place in honor of Reggie, Johnny, and my other children, then I have that responsibility. I felt called to share my story and the Method that I was using to help myself. It took me two solid years to get it all in writing, but I did.

At that point, I started my company, Mentally STRONG, as a small outpatient mental health clinic. I was the only provider and had a staff of one. I would teach people the Method in their counseling and medication management sessions. The practice started to grow very quickly because there is such a great need for mental health treatment in our community and all over the country. Although I was glad to be helping more and more people, the growth came with many stressors and frustrations too. I found out that running a business was extremely difficult and that there seemed to be so many obstacles standing in the way of sharing what I was really passionate about: sharing the Method to help others find mental strength.

Like always, I kept going. I learned how to handle finances and deal with medical insurance. I used to cry in my car before going into the clinic because it wasn't how I had envisioned helping others. I didn't want to manage people and run a private practice. But I continued to push through. After three years of immense setbacks and amazing growth, I now have four incredible Psychiatric Mental Health Nurse Practitioners and twelve Counselors that are helping over a hundred people per day become the best version of themselves. And we are continuing to grow and are continuing to develop the Mentally STRONG Academy in order to teach, train, and help as many people as possible. Our mission is to *empower all humanity to embrace the journey of mental strength*. And that mission includes you, me, and anyone else who is suffering.

CHAPTER THIRTEEN

COVID -19
and Caregiver Fatigue

It seemed that tragedy was everywhere in our lives, limited not just to our family but to our extended circle as well. I was in the kitchen of our beautiful Orlando resort room, surrounded by the ocean and celebrating my baby girl Miah's twenty-first birthday, when the phone rang. I was surprised that it was John, one of Bundy's good friends from college. Theirs was a tight knit group of guys who'd played football together. "Mike didn't make it," John said. My heart stopped. How would I tell Bundy? I considered not telling him. Yet, I knew that I couldn't do that. So, I paused for a moment before relaying the message. Bundy fell to the ground and let out a loud guttural noise. Everyone rushed into the kitchen to see what was wrong. Mike was Bundy's best friend, and they shared a deep connection.

Bundy and Mike were inseparable during those college years, and Mike always took care of Bundy, even as Bundy's condition had begun to worsen. It was an enormous blow to both of us. Mike had been there for Bundy and for me as well.

We'd known Mike's condition was bad but had still been hopeful. COVID-19 is so tricky. I had been in denial about the severity of it since the onset. It's just a virus, I told myself. It won't last long. I knew people who had contracted COVID-19, but they were mostly mild cases, and everyone ended up being fine.

Bundy was on a group call a few weeks earlier when John told all of them that Mike had been sick and tested positive for COVID-19. I pressed John to get more information. He told me, "Mike has been hospitalized because his respiratory symptoms are getting worse." I texted Mike immediately. "Why didn't you tell me?" I asked. "You have enough to deal with, I didn't want to bother you. I'll be okay" he said, and I believed him.

Mike was strong, in body and spirit, so we thought he'd fight it off and prayed for his healing. I'd planned the trip to Florida for Miah's birthday and stuck with our plans. I didn't tell Miah about Mike's condition because I didn't want her to worry.

She was very sensitive, having lost two brothers, and was so excited about her birthday. I didn't have the heart to dampen her mood. When I heard that Mike was put on a ventilator, I started to worry. As a nurse, I knew that losing Mike was a very real possibility, but I chose to believe that he would not die.

The family wrapped their arms around Bundy, while I tried to wrap my mind around the loss. Despite our continued vacation and celebration, all I could think about was the support Mike had given me over the last ten years. There'd been many phone calls, and Mike would even answer in the middle of the night if I needed him. "Mike, I can't handle this!" I'd sob into the phone as he attempted to comfort me. I was losing my husband and I was angry. Mike was angry too.

It was shortly after Reggie died, and Bundy and I were arguing about something stupid. All of the sudden, Bundy just snapped. He grabbed me and wouldn't let go. I tried to get away, squirming and screaming for help, but he had a solid grip. I managed to break free eventually and ran to our room, locking the door behind me. For the first time in twenty years of marriage, I was actually afraid of him. Bundy is a big and strong guy but had always been gentle with me. He was like this giant teddy bear who loved me. This more aggressive behavior was new, likely due to changes in his brain from the DRPLA. It seemed that I now needed help with Bundy, and Mike came to my rescue.

I probably spent an hour on the phone with Mike that day, telling him what happened and expressing my fear that Bundy would turn into an angry, abusive man. As always, Mike was able to comfort and encourage me. Mike called Bundy, upset with his friend. "Who the f**k do you think you are?" he said. I could hear the whole conversation. Mike ripped him a new one, and Bundy took it like a man. They were yelling, screaming, cussing, and crying for over an hour. The brotherly love those two men had for each other was like nothing I had ever experienced. The conversation, although intense, was also loving and supportive. "I love you, man!" Bundy said before he hung up.

"I love you too, a**hole. Now go apologize to your wife!"

Bundy did apologize to me and promised to work on his anger. Although his actions were grossly unacceptable, I understood why he was so angry. I was angry too. DRPLA was taking our beautiful family. I forgave him, but I needed some reassurance that it would never happen again. Mike offered to let Bundy stay with him in Maryland for a couple of weeks. He would open his home to Bundy whenever he was having a rough time. It was a grounding experience for Bundy, and he would come home feeling better.

Bundy called me from Mike's house in Maryland, genuinely apologetic. We had a long conversation, and I knew I could trust him to never hurt me again, but something was missing. I couldn't really connect with him emotionally, and I didn't know why. So, like always, after hanging up with Bundy, I called Mike.

"Thank you so much for your time with Bundy. I really appreciate it," I said. "As you know, he just called, and it was a really good conversation. He was the sweet and loving Bundy that would do anything for me. But I have to say…something was missing. I wasn't really able to connect with him emotionally like a husband and wife should. What is that?"

Mike gave me some details about their time together at his house, and it was becoming increasingly clear what Mike was trying to tell me. "I'm sorry Cristi, Bundy can't be that for you anymore." I had been thinking and complaining about my lack of connection with him for a couple of years, but I was having a hard time differentiating between normal twenty-five years of marriage stuff and DRPLA dementia. Mike confirmed my fears that day.

DRPLA was taking my relationship with my husband. If it wasn't for Mike, I don't know what my relationship with Bundy would have been like. Mike became my confidante when I had no one else to talk to about what I was going through with Bundy. I was experiencing extreme caregiver fatigue. The main issue for me was that I no longer felt that Bundy and I could have deep heartfelt conversations. Bundy was ever so slowly becoming regressively egocentric. I knew that it wasn't his fault, so I had to keep trying. Mike became my support, and we communicated frequently. I would confide in him about my frustrations with Miah and Bundy and work. I was able to talk to him openly about my fears for the future. Bundy repeatedly told both of us that he did not want to get to a point where someone had to take care of him.

There were several phone conversations that I had with Mike that started with questions like "What is going to happen when Bundy can't take care of himself?" We both didn't know the answer to that. It is a fact that DRPLA was going to take his ability to care for himself. A couple of times, we talked about Bundy's interest in Colorado's Right to Die law. I was very reluctant to discuss it with Bundy because I didn't want him to consider it. Mike had similar conversations with Bundy. I wondered what it would be like if Bundy had to go on hospice, but he's had such a slow progression, I've never been quite sure how to prepare.

Sometimes I've felt like I'm going crazy, because when I'm talking to my husband it starts to feel as if I'm talking to someone with dementia, but then his friends will tell me how impressed they are that he is doing so well. Do they not see what I see? Or is it twenty-five years of marriage, fear, and caregiver fatigue that has clouded my vision? Sometimes it's embarrassing. Mike confirmed that he could see it too, though. Bundy does really well when talking about things that he loves, like football, with so many old stories to tell. Not being around him every day, it's probably difficult for acquaintances to tell that his disease is progressing at all.

I still miss the conversations and support from Mike. He always gave me words of encouragement and called me super-woman. One day, he said something that I will never forget. I was complaining like I often do, not just about Bundy, but about how God was expecting too much from me. I told Mike that it wasn't fair that I no longer had a partner. He said, "You are Bundy's guardian angel. Any other woman would have left him years ago. God knew he had DRPLA, so He picked you for this amazing but difficult task. There is no doubt in my mind it's a task only you could do."

When I lost Mike, I lost my sounding board. There is no one else in this world who truly understands Bundy. If I could call Mike right now, and I wish I could, I would tell him all about what Bundy is up to now. Like how he is content watching TV and playing PlayStation, and how he has not let his anger get the best of him. Bundy loves when his children and grandchildren come to visit and share their candy and soda with him. Although I probably shouldn't have, I expressed to Bundy how I felt about him checking out as the head of our household after receiving his DRPLA diagnosis fifteen years ago. I told him that I've often felt like I had to fight this disease alone. Bundy didn't completely understand me, but he genuinely apologized for not being there to help during those difficult years. Mike would have been very proud of Bundy.

It's been twenty-five years with Bundy, and I wouldn't change my decision to marry him. I remember the feeling that I was experiencing God's love through him on our wedding day. I never worried about him desiring another woman. I have always known that he loves me more than anything in this world. His love has allowed me to be the best version of myself. Bundy always wanted to make me happy. When I said let's have children, let's be missionaries, let's adopt children, let's have more children, let's move to Colorado, he always said yes. He trusted me and I him. I have known from day one that this man would take a bullet for me without hesitation. And the bullets have been flying. I love you, Bundy.

CHAPTER FOURTEEN

Mermaid Miah

A lthough Mike's death put a shadow over Miah's birthday and there were fears about COVID, I knew how important that trip was for both Miah and me. I wanted to give my baby everything she ever wanted, including all the attention and love that she deserved. So, my sister and her family, Bundy, Miah, and I packed up and headed off to Orlando. We were going to hit Disney, followed by Universal Studios. Miah loves theme parks and roller coasters, especially Disney. I even signed us up for VIP tours at both parks so Miah would feel like a queen for her birthday.

Anyone who knows Miah knows that she loves mermaids, so much so that she wanted to be one. On the day of her birthday, we threw a family party, mermaid-themed, of course. My brother and his family were there, along with a few of our cousins. Miah's Aunt Sarah made her a gorgeous mermaid cake. It was three-tiered and covered with edible gold and glitter. All the bling on that cake made Miah smile from ear to ear. How she loves being with her family! We lounged in the sun and spent the day swimming at the resort's gigantic tropical pool. Miah had so much fun splashing in the waterfalls—like a mermaid herself. She'd learned to swim at a very early age, growing up in South Florida and having a Nana with a pool in her backyard. Miah was always a water baby and has gravitated to it ever since. It was a perfect day.

We headed to Disney World the following morning, meeting our tour guide outside of the park. They had a lot of rules, which I never like, so I was a little nervous that it would dampen our fun. I chose to make the best of it despite the restrictions, however, and it was amazing. We barely had to wait in line and were able to see Disney World, EPCOT, and Animal Kingdom all in one day! Universal Studios was even better with Harry Potter World and all the incredible roller coasters. Miah had her own personal tour guide at Universal, so we all felt like VIPs, but Miah was the most important VIP of all. The royal treatment made her day.

Before the trip, Miah had started a new experimental medication that reduced her seizures by 95 percent. Prior to that, it had always been difficult to get through vacations without a seizure ruining at least one or more days for Miah. I was so happy that for this entire trip, including roller coasters, parties, and late nights, we made it through the entire ten days without Miah having any grand mal seizures. This fact was even more exciting than Miah's birthday, which was already something monumental.

DRPLA had been taking Miah's abilities away slowly. When COVID hit, Miah had to withdraw from her program at the University of Colorado, Colorado Springs. It was designed for special needs adults to improve their independence. Although

Miah loved the social aspect, she could no longer complete the academics or walk around campus by herself. After leaving a school dance one day and having a wonderful time, the campus police stopped her. They thought she was an intoxicated college student because she was dancing on the sidewalk. That was the end of that!

In the five years after I lost Reggie, I did my best to balance feelings of anticipatory grief related to Miah with the urgency to live life to its fullest. Miah was happy, healthy, and still enjoying activities, but I couldn't help feeling triggered at times, wondering how long Miah would be with us. Sometimes Miah couldn't make it to the bathroom and could no longer attend to her personal hygiene. Sometimes she would fall when she was trying to do something or would tire easily, and her cognitive processing became painfully slow. We had multiple wheelchair evaluations as well as physical, speech, and occupational therapy appointments. Miah never wanted to sit in a wheelchair. Even when we purchased one specially customized for her, she refused to sit in it.

Miah loves spending time with people, engaging in a variety of activities. She enjoys anything that doesn't require exercise. I love the outdoors and often try to get Miah to hike, but the only outdoor activities that she likes are swimming and relaxing on a boat. She does enjoy spending my money, however, going out to eat or heading to a nail salon for a full-service manicure and pedicure.

I'm such a practical person that when I take Miah shopping and she requests all kinds of things that I think are ridiculous, I'm often puzzled. The majority of the time, I give in and buy her what she wants, though, mostly because I know that giving and receiving gifts is her love language. I giggle inside thinking about how I call her *Extra*. She always wants the rhinestones and sparkles.

Miah also loves going out to eat. When I take her to restaurants, I encourage a healthy meal and maybe a dessert. But because Miah adores sweets, I let her get whatever she wants. I think about how Reggie lost his ability to eat, and I want Miah to enjoy every minute of her life, including desserts. She will start with a brownie cake with whipped cream and eat the protein second. It isn't just that Miah is getting what she wants, it is the time spent, the love, and the true connection. I am her best friend, and she is my everything.

Of the many outings, Miah most cherishes shopping. We went to Build-a-Bear more than a few times, and she gathered a robust collection from those outings, along with gifts from her Aunt Jada.

After giving in to a new Build-a-Bear one day, we walked down the store aisles and spotted a Pegasus unicorn onesie with a tail. Miah looked at me and said, "Yes, we are definitely getting that!" I normally would have said no since I already got her a Build-a-Bear, but it was so cute and matched her personality so perfectly that I couldn't resist. Miah did not realize that it had a tail until we got home and she put it on. Then, she would not sit down because she was so excited about having a tail, walking around dancing and shaking it.

Miah adores all holidays and birthdays, but Christmas is by far her favorite. To celebrate Christmas 2021, Miah picked out a watch for Bundy during an online shopping spree. It was engraved with the words "Dad, no matter how much time passes, I'll always be your little girl." She also picked out a pocket mirror for me with the words "To my beautiful Mom. Never forget that I love you. Forever and always." She insisted that these were the best possible Christmas gifts for her parents, and she was right. We treasure them to this day.

Like me, Miah absolutely loves to travel. I remember taking her on a trip to New York City for her nineteenth birthday. She always wanted to see a show on Broadway, so we went to see *Chicago*. We spent the day there and did all the tourist things, like visiting the Statue of Liberty, the Empire State Building, and the 9/11 Memorial. But Miah's favorite part of New York was going to Madame Tussauds Wax Museum in Times Square, where she gave Usher a kiss, danced with Selena Gomez, modeled with Heidi Klum and Tyra Banks, had some girl time with Jennifer Lopez, shared superpowers with Captain Marvel, and hung out in the White House with President Barack Obama and his family. The two of us then danced the night away right there in the dance club.

Our travels didn't stop there, when our friend Heather asked us to go with her to Hawaii for work related to her Realm of Caring Fundraiser, we said yes immediately. It was an amazing time, cruising on a boat that stopped at the major islands of Oahu, Maui, Kauai, and the Big Island. We saw beautiful beaches and waterfalls, took a helicopter ride over an active volcano, and sunbathed on black sand beaches. We even got to hang out with Willie Nelson at his private home, where he signed guitars for the fundraiser. There was lots of family time, and the nights spent at the dance club were Miah's favorite.

Dancing is Miah's thing, and it's how she met her first love, Chris, at a dance party. Tim Tebow orchestrates and funds a dance for special needs adults around the country every February. It was at one of these dances that Miah caught the eye of a handsome young man who instantly fell in love. They danced, went for a limo ride, took pictures, and exchanged phone numbers at the end of the night. Little did I know that it would turn into a genuine long-term relationship. By the time of the same dance the following year, Chris and Miah were officially boyfriend and girlfriend, going on weekly dates and exchanging gifts regularly.

When they were coming up on their one-year anniversary, Chris asked for my permission to kiss Miah. I said, "Okay, but just a peck on the lips!" The intimacy never progressed past those innocent kisses and hand holding, but Chris made it very clear that his intention was to marry Miah one day. He promised to ask for my permission first but insisted that he wanted them to live together. I told him gently, "I think Miah will always have to live with me," to which he retorted, "That's fine. I'll move in with you!" When I relayed this story to his parents, we all laughed over the innocent but impractical request.

Miah also loves a good party and New Year's Eve is always a favorite. On December 31, 2020, we were in Daytona Beach at Miah's beach house. Before I bought the condo, I told Miah that I had been saving up for a down payment. She went into her room and pulled out $100 she had been saving and gave it to me. "Here, you can buy the beach house with this," she said. From then on, it was Miah's beach house, and she was proud of that fact.

We prepped for the New Year's celebration which is always fun with music, dancing, and lots of people. Miah was watching TV, dressed in sequins and a tiara, not wanting to rest before the party. Suddenly, I heard a loud thump, and went to check it out. Miah was lying on the floor, and blood was pouring from her mouth as she violently seized. I screamed for help from the family, put pressure on her lip, and held her on her side. I always go into nurse mode in these situations. Once the seizure had passed, I realized that she was going to need stitches. My sister and I drove her to the ER. There they stitched up the gash on her lip, and we made it back to the beach house before the celebrations at midnight.

The Fourth of July is another of Miah's most favorites. Why? The fireworks, of course. One Fourth, we took Miah to a reggae festival. She was decked out in red, white, and blue tie-dye and a sparkly red necklace. We got there early, grabbed some food and drinks, and sat out in the sun waiting for the band to start. It was too hot, though, and Miah began to seize. Something was different that time; the seizure seemed to last longer than usual.

I called 911 while I held on to Miah. Although the seizure was over by the time the paramedics got there, I felt uneasy. I had the paramedics transport her to Children's Hospital. Even though her tests were normal, she continued to scream in pain. The doctors thought it was seizure activity, so they gave her Versed, which did not help. After two hours of solid screaming, the doctor finally gave her morphine. Within twenty minutes, Miah was resting comfortably. That was the start of a new postictal state where she would need morphine after all her seizures. Poor Miah. I hated to see her in so much pain.

We fill as many days as we can with laughter and joy, and of course, I stand by Miah not only through the toughest moments brought on by her condition but also in the simplicity of the routine days as well. The first thing I always do every morning is to go and check on Miah. That morning was no different. I walked into her room with the mermaid-themed bedspread, stuffed animals everywhere, the bright mermaid on top of the window, and the same old mermaid barbies neatly placed in their usual spots. It was just as I had left it the night before, and so was Miah. She looked like she was resting peacefully in her mermaid paradise. Her CPAP was secure, and her left arm was strewn above her head. I didn't want to disturb her, so I let her sleep in as I continued with my normal morning routine.

When nurse Evevetta arrived, we went into Miah's room, but planned not to wake her, pulling the covers back only to do a mini assessment. I noticed what looked like a rash on the back of her left arm and then saw that it was on her right arm as well. "What is that?" I asked and started to shake her. She didn't respond.

I don't remember what I was thinking, but I began to panic, shaking her harder and harder "No!" I yelled. "No!" Her CPAP was securely on her face, so surely, she was still breathing. It was obvious that she had not had any seizure activity in the night. I would have been able to tell. Evevetta said, "She's not breathing!"

We tried to get the pulse-oximeter to work, and it seemed to be reading something. I thought I heard Evevetta's voice, "We have to start CPR." I called 911, and we pulled Miah to the floor, her body falling on the ground with a thud. I couldn't tell exactly what was happening, but we started CPR. Two breaths, five compressions. I gave two breaths, Evevetta gave five compressions. I was mad at the 911 operator who was telling me to calm down. "Is she breathing?" she asked. "We wouldn't be doing CPR if she was breathing," I snipped back at her. "Please, please send somebody!

This is not happening, I said to myself. *Rescue is going to get here and intubate her. I don't care if she needs to breathe out of a tube for the rest of her life, I just need her to live.* They had to get here to save her. Two breaths, five compressions. When Evevetta did the compressions, there was blood coming out of Miah's mouth. I was trying to get the suction machine to work between my breaths but couldn't. Two breaths, five compressions. Two breaths, five compressions. Two breaths, five compressions. The paramedics finally arrived.

Part of me knew that she was gone and part of me thought that they would save her. I texted my sister, "Miah's dead," even before I could bring myself to believe it. I don't think that they worked on her for that long, but I wasn't sure. I'd left the room. I couldn't handle it. I just couldn't fathom losing another child. I didn't want to see it, watch it, or hear it. I didn't want any of it.

Evevetta remained strong for both of us and stayed with Miah throughout. I sank to the ground on the sunroom floor and could hear the paramedic saying, "Where did her mom go?" I could hear them looking for me, but I couldn't speak. The paramedic came to me, saying what no mother should ever have to hear. "We did all that we could... she's dead." I didn't move. I didn't speak. I was glued to that sunroom floor, sun in my eyes and pain in my heart.

Evevetta took over managing the scene. The family began arriving, but the rest is blurry. I do recall thinking about the day Reggie died. When it happened, I was in so much shock that I did not touch him, hug him, or say goodbye to his physical body. Remembering that, I leapt up from the ground. I wasn't going to let that happen twice. "I have to be with her," I cried. I spent the next several hours lying next to her lifeless body as family, friends, police officers, paramedics, and others came in and out of the room. I didn't care. I was holding my baby for the last time, and nobody was going to tell me otherwise.

CHAPTER FIFTEEN

Let It Matter

We had three celebrations of life for Miah to make sure that everyone who loved her got to have one last dance with her. I'm sure that Miah approved. One thing about Miah is that she loved Jesus but hated sitting through a church service. It was only fitting then that there was no memorial for Miah, only parties. Even amongst COVID fears, flocks of people came out to celebrate her life. I know that she was watching over us while the DJ played loud music, so we gave her a show. We danced in our formal wear, tears rolling down our cheeks. We loved on one another, gave out lots of hugs, and carried on just as if Miah were the hostess. I'm sure she would have thrown confetti and glitter down from heaven if she could.

As I began to grieve, I spent most of my time being angry at God. I asked Him, "*Why?*" I am a mentally and emotionally strong person, but the pain and the anger are still overwhelming at times. I spent hours meditating and listening for an answer, hoping for Him to tell me what to do or how to go on.

In the midst of it all, I had an experience with Miah similar to the one I'd had with Reggie. I could feel her there and asked her, "Miah, where are you?" She said, "I'm right here, Mommy!" I was overcome with a feeling that she is filled with divine contentment. I knew in that moment that time and space are a limitation of human experience. That was the beginning of my understanding of the eternal relationship that I have with my children. It was not the end of my pain, however. I had never experienced this type of intuition, and I didn't know what to do with it. I was also in so much emotional pain that I had to take time to care for myself.

Who am I, how do I grieve, and how do I turn this unbearable pain into purpose? I am first and foremost Cristi, then Dr. B. I am a sensitive woman, a friend, a mom who has lost three children, and a wife who has become a caretaker for her husband. At the same time, I am also a mental health professional, an expert in grief, and the owner of the Mentally STRONG brand. The pressure on me to not have a breakdown is pretty damn high. To be honest, I *really want* to have a breakdown. I've been through a lot, and I don't want to care. I want someone to rescue me, just like in the movies. In these moments, I must tell myself what I often tell others: *No one is going to rescue you. This is not a movie. You are the only one that can do this for yourself. You must find the strength within.* That's why I developed the Mentally STRONG Method. It has helped me so much and continues to help me and many others too.

After my daughter Miah died, I chose to grieve publicly with a video blog because I wanted to be vulnerable and share what I was going through with others. I also decided to do a Mentally STRONG Method session in front of my entire staff with ounselor input. It started off as a training session for them, but it was also empowering for me because I was able to receive new insights about myself.

I was anxious as I sat in front of the twenty-five staff who looked up to me as their leader. I was afraid to show any weakness, but at the same time, I knew that was exactly what I was supposed to do. We started just like any other Mentally STRONG Method session would begin in the office, by using a Thought Map. A Thought Map is a worksheet that helps you identify your central thought or feeling as well as anything related to that feeling. My central thought that day was pain. I chose pain because what I felt was more than sadness, more than grief, and yet different from depression. Unbearable pain was the best way to describe what I was experiencing. I often describe working on a Thought Map as twenty years of journaling in twenty minutes. It brings thoughts to the surface so that they can be processed and dealt with in a healthy manner. The following concepts came out during my Thought Map session:

- I am experiencing unbearable pain from grief.

- I thought I had more time with Miah. (Anger with God)

- I thought if I served God, my family would be protected. (Anger with God)

- I never experienced trauma like performing CPR on my dead child. (Fear)

- I am to blame; I was the caretaker at the time of both Reggie and Miah's deaths. (Shame)

- How am I supposed to trust God or even myself. (Shame)

- This changed my life and my identity. All I ever wanted to be was a mom. (Shame)

- I wanted to be in a story where I found a cure and we lived happily ever after. (Anger with God)

- I wasn't good enough, smart enough, or persistent enough. (Negative thoughts going back to my childhood.)

Doing the Thought Map publicly was the most vulnerable thing I could have done during my early grief. To be authentic, I had to admit my underlying core connections, negative thoughts, and all of the other feelings that were impacting my ability to heal.

Next, I had to organize those thoughts into bite-sized actions that I could then make choices about. I use ten categories to organize my thoughts and feelings. Here are just a few that I was struggling with that day:

- Grief

- Trauma

- Anxiety

- Behaviors and Choices

- Negative Thoughts

- Spiritual Conflict

Grief/Trauma. I chose to grieve because I know that Controlled Grief is effective. I scream for help, but no one can help me. Imagine someone you love burning in a fire and you can't save them. You try your hardest, but they die, and you are left to live. That's me, I've been trying to save my family from the fire of DRPLA for fifteen years but couldn't. The pain is so deep, so final, so heavy. I don't even know where to start. I thought for a moment in meditation and challenged God. *You said that Jesus felt everything we felt, show me.*

There is a story in the garden of Gethsemane that I looked up in the Bible. "…My soul is exceeding sorrowful, even unto death…." (Matthew 26:38, *King James Version*). Those were Jesus's words. He wasn't suicidal, nor am I, but that is the only way to describe this pain. I know it is important to keep grief in a separate category; otherwise, it will spill into every area of my life. Unfortunately, there is no way to fix grief. I believe in Controlled Grief, so I am choosing to take the time to feel this pain a little bit at a time.

Anxiety/Worry. I am not typically an anxious person, or at least I didn't think so. However, in this session, a lot of anxiety came to the surface. As I have chosen to grieve publicly, I have a fear of judgment from others—judgment from Christians that might say that I'm not doing things according to their understanding of God, and even from non-Christians who might say that I talk about God too much. People may even say that I'm too emotional or not emotional enough. I know that I shouldn't care about what other people think, but I do.

I also uncovered a lot of anxiety about where I will be in the next four to six months. I may be putting an unrealistic expectation on myself in terms of the grief process and thinking that I will be farther along than is possible for me and that I will be a much stronger person then. At the end of the day, my biggest worry is my husband. His DRPLA is worse than where Miah's was but not as bad as Reggie's. I worry about what's going to happen with his medical condition and his ability to function.

In each category, I challenge myself to choose a positive reaction, as difficult as it may be. I call this the Power of Choice. I choose to control the way I react to my anxiety. I choose to trust myself, the Mentally STRONG Method, and my support system.

Behaviors and Choices. The category of behaviors and choices is separate and reserved for maladaptive behaviors. We all have maladaptive behaviors or coping mechanisms. Even though I have done a lot of self-development, in a time like this, it is very possible to regress to previous behaviors. I had an eating disorder in my early twenties (bulimia nervosa) and some continued disordered eating behaviors into later adulthood. I talk about this openly on my YouTube Channel and I continue to make progress in this area. I eat healthy, try to exercise, and do not purge my food. However, under extreme stress, I sometimes binge, feel guilty, and am constantly worried about weight and dieting. Knowing that this year of grief is going to be my hardest yet, I must make some choice to protect myself from regression.

Another maladaptive coping behavior I see frequently in my professional practice is people turning to alcohol as a way of coping. Grief is extreme pain, and I would be lying if I said that alcohol or other numbing substances don't temporarily help with that pain. Like many people with trauma, I am having trouble sleeping. My mind won't stop thinking about death, and relaxing seems impossible. I can see how anyone in such a state can get to the point of using substances too much. There-fore, my choice is to put "rules" in place for myself and around my behavior. For example, I have decided to never drink alone and to not drink every day. Those are my rules, and I have chosen to stick with them for my own self-preservation.

Another form of maladaptive behaviors and choices is placing unrealistic expectations on myself, others, or the time needed to accomplish things. My team challenged me to acknowledge that I had a lot of internal dialogue that was inappropriate guilt and that I was expressing some *all-or-nothing* thinking. Ultimately, I have an unrealistic expectation that I can save everyone. Using the Power of Choice, I choose to remind myself to manage my expectations, to acknowledge my intelli-gence, and to show up and reach for support.

Negative Thoughts. Everyone needs to know that how you talk to yourself has a significant impact on your mood. Changing negative thoughts into positive thoughts is the basis of the self-help industry and many talk-therapy sessions. Learning to do this for yourself is an important part of personal growth. Honestly, I can tell you, though, that it's easier said than done. I have been working on improving myself using cognitive behavioral tech-niques for close to thirty years, and specifically the Mentally STRONG Method for almost fifteen years, and I still recognize a pattern of those negative thoughts. I call them Core Connections.

Depending on what is going on in my life, I have a theme of negative internal dialogue and have learned to use effective reframing to minimize its impact on my mood. After Miah's death, losing all my biological children and one of my adopted children, and not feeling like I was the best mother to any of my adopted children, my internal dialogue was screaming: *You are a failure at being a mother. Motherhood is one of the most important roles in your life, and you failed. No other accomplishment matters!*

Now comes the choice, which is my power or weakness. I can choose to listen to that voice and find all the evidence that those negative statements are true, or I can find the positive. I can use evidence from my life to talk myself out of this negative thought. For example, I spent years researching and implementing all different types of treatments and modalities for Reggie. I continued to support the girls by getting them into programs and helping them through their darkest times. I never gave up on any of my children. I was constantly searching to find a cure for DRPLA, and in the midst of all of that, I was able to still find time to do fun things with my kids and to continue to enjoy life. I gave them a family, a support system, and traditions, even when it was challenging to do so.

After all that, still another deep, negative thought comes into my mind: *you did your best, but your best wasn't good enough.* Therefore, my Core Connection is that I am not good enough. What do I do with the negative thought of *I'm not good enough*? That thought runs so deep and started in my early childhood. It seems to always come up regardless of what I am dealing with, so I acknowledge it, reframe it, and let it go. Since there is an unrealistic expectation in my mind to be perfect, I will never be good enough.

Negative versus positive self-talk is such a big part of self-development, mood, and ultimately, mental strength. It is also a lifetime process improvement. The more I practice reframing negative thoughts and fostering positive thinking, the easier it becomes. Acknowledging when difficult things happen in life, even old patterns can reemerge. I believe that insight equals confidence, and, in this process, you can see some of my old patterns. You can also see me reframing, finding the positive, and choosing to believe in myself.

Spiritual Conflict. As you can imagine, I continue to struggle with my relationship with God. How could God possibly love me and yet take my children away from me? Those two things seem so distant and so far apart from each other. I can't wrap my mind around how God could allow it to happen. Even with all of the pain, anger, and blame toward God, I know, in my heart, that I am committed to never giving up on having a true and authentic spiritual relationship with Him. In my over-whelming grief after the loss of my daughter, I have committed to researching and participating in spiritual traditions that are outside my comfort zone, ones that I believe can bring me closer to God.

I took part in a traditional Lakota Sweat Lodge Ceremony that was profound. The four rounds that I participated in allowed me to feel closer to God, to Miah, and to my purpose on earth. I spent the day in mental and emotional preparation. It was a New Moon, and I went with the intention to let go of my anger. I had been very angry that Miah died without warning and that I have now lost Johnny, Reggie, and Miah. I was also angry that my husband is no longer an emotional partner.

When I arrived at the land keeper's home, I was greeted with so much warmth and concern. But I was having difficulty breathing and was unable to talk about my intentions because I was so filled with grief and weighed down with a heavy heart. During the first round, I meditated on what "spirit" I was going to bring into the ceremony. I quickly remembered my encounters with Reggie and Miah who had both expressed a supernatural contentment, and I meditated on the spirit of contentment.

During my second round, my prayer was to release my anger, and I prayed not to be an angry person. Others prayed for me and shared their spiritual experiences that were directly related to Reggie and Miah. The third round was the most profound of all. I felt content and even danced a little. That is something that Miah and I share, a love for dancing, and it helped me feel closer to her. My final round was grounding, and I was extremely thankful for the experience.

I believe that there is a spiritual relationship waiting for everyone, and I continue to commit to the thought that if I authentically look, I will find it. I am learning that it doesn't have to be inside my own culture or religious upbringing. When I first created The Mentally STRONG Method, my last question was "How does this impact your relationship with God?" After three years of using the Method in a professional setting, I realized that many people have what is commonly called "church trauma" as it relates to what they have experienced or been taught about God. Therefore, I recently changed the question to "How does this impact your spiritual relationship?" I believe mental strength comes from mind, body, and spirit, and will continue to choose to challenge and develop my authentic spiritual relationship.

Insight and Personal Vision. One of the advantages of allowing myself to be vulnerable during a Mentally STRONG Method session that day with my staff is that I received insight from several counselors. That is another benefit of professional counseling or working through the Mentally STRONG Method with someone to guide you. I have many years of professional experience and personal growth, yet the counselors were able to identify some things that I had never connected with before. One of the Mentally STRONG counselors shared her insight that starting in my childhood, I took on the idea that *it's all on me.* She uncovered that I was always searching for how to be good enough, but I then had all my negative thoughts and core connections confirmed through the grief and trauma that I experienced. She also noted that in my behaviors and choices I have been overcompensating with achievements and that I continue to overcompensate after "failing" by trying to save everyone.

I want to keep empowering myself, but my personal vision is to also empower others to confidently say "I am Mentally STRONG." I will continue to share my story and the Mentally STRONG Method as an effective tool to think, organize, and choose. But, as I was reminded of that day, it can't be "all on me." My entire team gave me the permission to give myself grace, mercy, and the time to heal. And I am still healing, but I continue to grow stronger every day. I hope you've also thought about how to "Let It Matter" in your life.

CHAPTER SIXTEEN

Purpose

As hard as it is to say, I must believe that Johnny, Reggie, and Miah have each fulfilled their purpose. I keep physical reminders around me all the time, including carrying their ashes with me. I have turned them into diamonds, one of which represents my wounded heart, worn through a dermal piercing. Miah's ashes are also in a lotus flower around my neck, and Reggie's are on my bracelet. Additionally, I often remember the Christmas gifts that Miah purchased just before her death and will forever hold the engraved words precious, "To my beautiful Mom. Never forget that I love you. Forever and always."

As I look back on the impact that my children had on myself and others, it gives me the strength and desire to fulfill my purpose. Reggie left an imprint on many people, and Miah left behind fond memories and the trinkets she'd collected over the years. Everyone that came to honor Miah at her celebrations was asked to take their favorite toys, jewelry, stuffed animals, or items of clothing. Many walked away with their favorite Build-a-Bears to display so that they could cherish their relationship with Miah forever. And remember that Pegasus unicorn onesie with the tail? Miah's friend Jennifer is now the proud owner and frequently sends me pictures when she wears it. It means a lot to me to know that Miah is remembered. I am a mother bearing unbearable grief, but I feel joy when reminiscing about the feelings, the life, and love that my children brought into the world.

Johnny's purpose appeared so briefly in my life, but Johnny was there for his sisters when they needed him. They looked up to him and clung to him during those early times of trouble. He was the one who led them to a safe and loving home. Johnny brought them to me, and I will be forever grateful to him for that. He was the first of my children to teach me about compassion and loss. Although I had the least amount of time with him, he showed me so much. Johnny also helped prepare me for the rest of the heartache that would follow and for the eventual loss of Reggie and Miah.

Reggie's purpose was profound and touched hundreds of people's lives. Naturally charming, he was born with all the character traits he would need for his life's purpose. Reggie was extremely persistent, and I quickly learned that childproof did not mean Reggie-proof. As things got more difficult for him, he persisted and never gave up. Reggie found his passions at a very early age, and nothing could sway him from playing ball, running fast, and, of course, embracing the role of his favorite, friendly, neighborhood masked avenger. Those passions would always give him joy, no matter what.

Reggie was born strong and resilient. He needed that strength and called upon it daily, showing his resilience time and time again. Reggie also taught me how to find those traits within myself and how to hope even when there is no hope.

When I consider the number of people who were strangers initially but repeatedly drove long distances to be with him, it's obvious that Reggie was a rare and special person who was dearly loved by many. It was not uncommon for me to hear people say that Reggie made everyone a better person. Without words, he taught them the meaning of hope and love, the value and significance of touch, how to live with purpose, and the worth of being present in the moment. Reggie inspired thankfulness, gratitude, and service. So many people said that when they were with Reggie, they felt like they were in the presence of an angel. And let's not forget his infectious smile that could brighten anyone's day. My father even went so far as to say, "Reggie taught me how to suffer like a man." What a powerful tribute!

Reggie's purpose was clear to all who knew him. To me, he was my first love, my greatest challenge, and he taught me more than words can describe. I often refer to the letter that I wrote to Reggie shortly after his death. In it, I admitted that it would be selfish to want him back on this earth for myself (but I still do). When Reggie spoke to me after his death, he said, "Momma, you think you are so smart, but you have no idea. I'm okay. Dad and Miah are okay. And you will be okay." Little did I know that I would eventually learn to have an eternal relationship with my children.

And then there was Miah. Although many people loved Miah, I believe that her life's purpose and impact are eternally specific to me. She lived in the same way in which she died, peacefully. Miah didn't pull hundreds of people together, but when she had people around her, they felt her utter sweetness, peace, and love for all. That was her personality from the day she was born. My perfect baby grew into a perfect child, happily living in the shadow of adventurous and strong-willed Reggie with his big personality and intense illness. Miah was always present, though, and did not require a lot of attention. She only wanted those around her to be happy and to feel loved.

There is nothing like experiencing tragedy after tragedy to break down your perception of reality and to further push you to break down mentally and emotionally. Miah's death was the event that shattered everything for me because I wasn't ready. I wanted answers. I was wounded but still open to whatever God had to offer. Although I knew that there was a God, I needed more than the empty promises that I felt from Him while reading the Bible. I longed to hear from Him directly. I had to know why and ached to understand my eternal relationships. I refused to shut down or block out the possibility of being able to continue to communicate with my children. Reggie clearly spoke to me after his death and then Miah. I knew I had to hold on to that gift.

When I concentrated on it, I immediately felt connected to Miah like she was right there with me. I would just envision her standing on my left with her head on my shoulder. Then, as I grew bolder, I would speak to her. In the beginning, she would just say things like, "Mama, I'm right here," or "Mama, I'm okay." I never wrote a letter to Miah because I felt like I could talk to her and didn't need to write. Honestly, I would often fight with myself over it, arguing that I was just making these interactions up to feel better about losing her.

As I was going through the grief process and trying to trust that I was eternally connected to Miah, I chose to consult a medium. I was thrilled when the medium confirmed the intuitive experiences that I was having with Miah and God. I began to practice conversing with Miah, Reggie, other eternal relationships, and, of course, with God directly. God has spoken to my heart and told me that this ability is my gift. He understands my pain and has given me this aptitude so that my soul can understand and my heart can heal.

Of course, as any mother would, I had to ask Miah why. *Why did you have to die?* Miah told me that she had a choice that night. God came to her and revealed her purpose in the next life but told Miah that she could choose whether or not to go at that time. It was up to her. Miah decided that she did not want to experience the things that Reggie went through: the pain, the extreme physical limitations, or the inability to talk, walk, or communicate. So, she chose to go. Miah understood that leaving would hurt me and that I would miss her terribly, so she asked for my forgiveness. Of course, I immediately told her that I forgave her, but sometimes the pain is still too much. In those moments, I feel so selfish because I want her back. But it is also in those moments that she reminds me, "I'm right here, Mommy."

The fact that she had a choice was confirmed by Maddie, one of Miah's friends. She told me that Miah speaks to her through a song from their favorite movie. I went home to listen to the lyrics. I laid down on Miah's bed crying, while playing the song on repeat. Miah spoke to me through it as well. She said that she didn't belong here and that she had to go. It was the best choice for her and would allow her to fulfill her ultimate purpose. How can I argue with my own daughter in her mature eternal state? And so, Miah's purpose lives on.

On another occasion when Miah was speaking to me, she said something that will stick with me forever. She said, "Reggie's purpose was to get you to a place, and mine is to stay with you forever." It is so true that Reggie got me to many places: mentally, emotionally, spiritually, and even physically with the move to Colorado. Aggressively fighting for Reggie 's life and fervently praying for his healing, traveling the world and moving my family across the country for him to ultimately die, brought me to a place. It was a place that needed mental, emotional, and spiritual healing. Although Miah's death nearly broke me, I now know that we are together forever, eternally connected and able to communicate.

Miah helps me when I'm struggling. One of my current struggles is my relationship with Bundy. We are grieving so differently. I grapple with the question: Are we growing apart or is he experiencing dementia related to DRPLA? As I talk with Miah, she reminds me that she was Daddy's girl, that he loved her the most, and that his heart is very broken. It's too bad, but Bundy is not able to connect with her on a spiritual level. Miah clearly told me, "He'll understand it all, though, when he gets here." I asked her what I should do in the meantime, in terms of our relationship. She said, "Love him like he loves me, simple and solid." And so, I try.

Since Miah's death, I have been experiencing PTSD symptoms during the night and first thing in the morning. As part of my treatment for them, I participated in ketamine hypnosis therapy. The goal for me doing so was to uncover a place where I could use self-guided imagery to find relaxation and contentment during my everyday life. Using this method, I was able to find an imaginary place that works for me and go there whenever I want; it's a floating dock on a calm ocean near a tropical island. I lay on the floating dock with the sun beaming on my skin. Miah lies next to me, while Reggie playfully swims in the distance. Having this designated place where I can feel the peaceful presence of my children gives me the strength to handle anything.

It is hard to believe and even harder to accept that one of my adopted children and both of my biological children have fulfilled their purposes before me. It is so unnatural to lose a child, but to lose three brings unimaginable pain. To honor Johnny, Reggie, and Miah's purpose, I need to also acknowledge and honor mine. I will "Let it Matter" by continuing to not only share their stories but also the story of how I found the strength to live out my purpose. And I believe that it's working.

I know my willingness to share is appreciated and will continue to help people. I am not saying that it is easy. It is extremely hard and takes my willingness to feel and work through the pain and to acknowledge the depressed mood that comes along with that. When I feel down, I use elements of the Mentally STRONG Method to think, organize, and choose how to process those feelings and find joy. Honestly, sometimes the choice for me is just to be sad, cry, and not be productive that day, and that's okay. It's a time-limited choice that I call Controlled Grief.

Sometimes, I choose to read testimonies about how my life and perseverance has helped others. In those instances, I am choosing to accept my purpose, turning my pain into strength as part of my healing. I hope that sharing my story, my family, and my life has impacted you for the better. The process of putting it all down on paper has been painful, invigorating, and given some purpose to my grief and sadness. At the end of the day, I am a mother who has loved, and always will love, all of her children: Johnny, Reggie, Miah, Nidra, Cory, Kayla, and Cristina. I will forever miss those that I can no longer hold and will cling tightly to our eternal relationship, while cherishing those who are still here.

Every good book has a happy ending, and mine is this: I am forever blessed to be the mother that I am. I get to tell my children's stories over and over. I have also been given a gift where I am able to experience the reality of eternal relationships. That is priceless, and that is my happy ending.

For all the hardship that I have been through, I would not take a single day back. If God allowed me a do-over and asked me, "Do you want Johnny, Reggie, and Miah even if they are going to die an early death all over again?" I would without a doubt say, "*YES.*" My happy ending is knowing my purpose and uncovering my ability to be vulnerable. I am not ashamed of my shameful thoughts. I know that by sharing both the good and bad of my pain and purpose, other people will be able to find their purpose. Don't feel sorry for me because I have lost my children. My soul is eternal, and I have been blessed to see the glimpse of it through my eternal relationship with Miah by my side.

I will always be a mother, but I am also a friend, an advocate, and a child of God who wants to see others thrive in this world. I have come to understand, more so now than ever, that my life's work is to help others grow in mental strength. I'm hopeful that you saw bits of your own story in mine and that you've realized that you are not alone in your suffering. Human connections are what we all need to be inspired to keep going another day, even when those days are tough (and they will be). But always remember, there are lots of good times too, and that you have the power to choose. So please, for me, for Reggie, for Miah, and for Johnny, choose love, choose joy, choose family, choose hope, and choose to never give up. Whatever your story, whatever your pain, there is a way to find peace. If I can do it, you can do it. Never give up on turning your pain into purpose.

Discussion Questions

Prologue

Cristi shared her Why in the prologue. Have you ever contemplated what your Why is? What has been your path to Mental Strength?

Chapter 1

The family reunion was the tipping point of tragedy for Cristi. What tragedy does this bring up from your life? How did you initially respond to that tragedy?

Chapter 2

Has there ever been a time in your life when you felt like everything was perfect only to have the rug pulled out from under you like Cristi did?

It is common in grief to try to find meaning in death. Think about a loss that you've experienced. Have you been able to find meaning for it as Cristi was trying to do in the last paragraph?

Chapter 3

Even as a nurse, Cristi felt fear and confusion when trying to determine what was happening with her son (medically. Have you ever felt fear and confusion as it relates to a medical diagnosis?

How does a medical diagnosis change someone's life? The lives of those around them?

Chapter 4

It's challenging to be a parent. In what ways can you relate to Cristi and Bundy's interactions with their adopted daughters?

Chapter 5

Do you think the diagnosis revealed in this chapter helped or hindered Cristi? In what ways?

How did Cristi find positivity? In what ways can you find positivity in your own hardships?

Chapter 6

A lot of heavy things were happening in this chapter. What do you think it would have been like to be Cristina during this time? Cristi? Can you relate to this experience?

Chapter 7

This chapter is titled *Hope vs. Hopelessness*. What do you think the difference is? In what ways did Cristi choose hope? In what ways can you choose hope?

Chapter 8

This chapter talks about Reggie addicts. What was in it for the participants of Reggie therapy?

How has it felt for you when you've helped others?

Chapter 9

Medical marijuana is a controversial topic. What are your thoughts about it? Would you have made a similar move for your family?

Chapter 10

This chapter is about sacrificing for others. What sacrifices did Bundy and Cristi make? What sacrifices have you made for your family and others?

Chapter 11

This is a very painful chapter. Cristi had an obvious loss, but what else did she lose on that day?

Have you ever fought/prayed so hard and wanted something so badly (like Cristi did) only to have it not work out? What impact did that experience have on your relationship with God? With yourself? How did it change you?

Chapter 12

What is meant by the quote "with great power comes great responsibility?" As it relates to Cristi's story? As it relates to your own story?

Have you ever taken a tragedy from your life and created something good from it?

Chapter 13

Can you relate to the notion of caregiver fatigue? What might this have felt like for Cristi?

Who do you support and who supports you during difficult times?

Chapter 14

Even though Miah is special and has a neurodegenerative diagnosis, how is she impacting others?

Chapter 15

What do you think about Cristi's decision to create the Mentally Strong Method? How did it help her? How can it help you?

Chapter 16

Hopefully your story is not as tragic as Cristi's. Everyone, however, has a story. What is your story and how are you going to find purpose in it?

Engaging and Empowering

re you looking for a speaker who will leave your audience motivated to be their very best? Dr. Bundukamara is a dynamic speaker who is turning her pain into purpose, whose story is so powerful your audience can't help but engage.

Invite Cristi Bundukamara, EdD PMHNP to Speak to Your Organization

Topics Include but are not limited to:

- The Mentally STRONG Method
- Grief to Growth: Navigating Your Journey
- Become More Successful by Unlocking Your Emotional Wealth
- Think, Organize & Choose: The Secret of Mental Strength

Contact **Cristi Bundukamara** today for a customized speaking presentation. She specializes in motivational speaking, keynote speaking and large group presentations

www.CristiBundukamara.com

Follow Cristi Bundukamara on Social Media

Mentally Strong Academy

At the Mentally STRONG Academy, we empower individuals to unlock their inner resilience, cultivate mental strength, and transform their lives. Founded by the esteemed Cristi Bundukamara, EdD PMHNP, our academy is dedicated to providing a comprehensive and empowering approach to mental strength through evidence-based practices rooted in Cognitive Behavioral Therapy (CBT).

Our mission is simple yet profound: to inspire all humanity to embrace the journey of mental strength

The Mentally STRONG Method: Our cornerstone approach, the Mentally STRONG Method, is firmly rooted in CBT principles. CBT is a highly effective therapeutic technique that focuses on changing negative thought patterns and behaviors, empowering individuals to overcome many challenges.

Diverse Programs: We offer a range of programs to cater to diverse needs. Whether you're seeking personal growth, professional development, or the ability to support others in your community, we have a program for you.

- Access our comprehensive online courses from the comfort of your own home, designed to help you master the Mentally STRONG Method at your own pace.

- Become a certified Mentally STRONG Coach through our intensive training program. Equip yourself with the skills to guide others on their journey to mental strength.

- Join our customized Ambassador Program, designed to empower you to make a positive impact in your community.

At the Mentally STRONG Academy, we believe that mental strength is the foundation for achieving your fullest potential. Join us on a transformative journey to become the best version of yourself and help others do the same. Discover the power of the Mentally STRONG Method and embark on a path to a brighter, more resilient future.

www.MentallyStrongAcademy.com

Dr. Cristi Bundukamara, EdD PMHNP is a distinguished psychiatric nurse practitioner with over two decades of dedicated expertise. Her journey into the world of healthcare began as an Army Medic, setting the foundation for a career defined by compassion and unwavering commitment.

A pivotal point in her educational journey led her to Florida International University, where she earned a Master's degree in Psychiatric Nursing. With a passion for elevating the standards of mental health care, Cristi Bundukamara pursued a doctorate in Healthcare Education, solidifying her position as a thought leader in the field.

Cristi Bundukamara's groundbreaking work culminated in the establishment of the pioneering Mentally STRONG Clinic in the vibrant community of Colorado Springs, CO. Here, she harnessed her extensive experience and visionary approach to mental health, transforming the lives of countless individuals.

Not content with revolutionizing clinical practice alone, Cristi Bundukamara went on to found the Mentally STRONG Academy, a hub of learning and empowerment. Cristi Bundukamara's passion for fostering mental strength shines through her empowering books and workbooks and captivating speaking engagements. Her dynamic presentations offer profound insights into the art of processing emotions, coupled with practical strategies for cultivating mental strength.